Teddy Bear a

Stroll through a century of talking therapies

Gerald Alan Fox

GERALD ALAN FOX

Gerald Alan Fox has asserted his rights under the Copyright, Designs and Patents Act 1988 to be identified as the author of this work.

ISBN: 9781092691000
Imprint: Independently published

BISAC: Non-fiction/Psychotherapy

First published in Great Britain in 2019 by Gerald Alan Fox.

Copyright © Gerald Alan Fox 2019

A CIP catalogue record for this book is available from The British Library.

All rights reserved.

No part of this publication may be produced, stored in a retrieval system, or transmitted in any form, or by any means, without the prior permission in writing of the publisher, nor be otherwise circulated in any form of binding or cover other than that in which it is published and without a similar condition including this condition being imposed on the subsequent publisher.

Grateful acknowledgement is made for kind permission to use lines from the songs:

You are my Sunshine Co-written by Jimmie Davis and Charles Mitchell. First recorded in 19 39 on the Decca label

Me and my Teddy Bear

Co-written by J. Fred Coots and Jack Winters
Lyrics © Warner/Chappell Music, Inc.

Guy who found the Lost Chord

Co-written by jiimmy Durante and Earl K. Brent. Released as a single on the MGM label in 19 64.

My Bonnie lies over the Ocean

Is a traditional Scottish folk song from the 18th Century.

The Teddy Bears' Picnic

Music by John Walter Bratton, 1907. Lyrics by Jimmy Kennedy, 1932.

Dedicated to all arctophiles

(People who adore, treasure or collect Teddy bears. Gr. *Arktós*/bear, *philos*/friend)

Acknowledgements:

I gratefully thank my editor, David Willis and proof reader, Jeremy Tatham.

Cover: Formatted by Dr D.N.A. Fox, sketches by Rex da Golf.

Also by the same author:

A Bird Stuck on the Sky (2014)

TEDDY BEAR AND FREUD

Me and my Teddy Bear

In the house next door right next to mine
A little boy lives there
At Xmas time dear Santa Claus
Brought him a Teddy bear

He loves his little Teddy bear
He's with it all day long
And the sweetest thing I've ever heard
Is to hear him sing this song

Me and my Teddy bear
Have no worries, have no cares
Me and my Teddy bear
Just play and play all day

I love my Teddy bear
He has one eye and has no hair
But I love my Teddy bear
We play and play all day

Every night he's with me
When I climb up the stairs
And by my bed he listens
Until I say my prayers

Oh, me and my Teddy bear
Have no worries, have no cares
Me and my Teddy bear
Just play and play all day

CHAPTER ONE

One never quite gets over a lost bear. Jane Swan

An easyJet pilot arrived at his aircraft early one morning. He went through his routine before flying. As he glanced into the cabin he spotted a sad-looking bear staring back at him from the aisle floor. Seemingly dropped or left behind from the last flight of the previous day, the bear – named Shackleton – must have been lost during the rush to disembark. The pilot took on the challenge.

'Until Shackleton is claimed, Captain Clutterbuck is flying around the airline's network with the bear, taking pictures of him in the destinations he flies to and keeping a log book of his travels. So far the bear has been to Reykjavik, Copenhagen, Belfast and Bordeaux among other stops. He was most likely left on the Bordeaux to Luton flight on 20th December 2016.'

This story was issued on 12th January 2017 by the media centre at easyJet, and featured on ITV and in several newspapers. The airline took to Facebook and Twitter with the hashtag #GetShackletonHome, in the hope of finding its owner.

Many people are inclined to react strongly to minor dramas such as this one. Perhaps you admired the pilot or felt sorry for the unknown child, or even imagined offering to adopt the lost Teddy yourself?

You may have had similar experiences as a child or parent. Why do we attach so much importance to what, superficially, is such a trivial misfortune? Have you ever considered why you clung to your bear? If you presented a child with a Teddy did you consider any consequences?

Many children become emotionally attached to a soft toy. Things don't go well if it's mislaid, particularly at bedtime. Major repercussions can result if it's truly lost. Why? It's only a toy. Try to replace it at your peril.

Some strangers like the easyJet pilot may make every conceivable effort to reunite a child with their Teddy. Parents – harangued or otherwise – will take on arduous searches to find lost bears. It's instinctive. When children lose a special companion they can suffer deeply. Why?

The reasons are complex. I speak from experience. I lost my Teddy bear at a young age. He was irreplaceable. It took me years to come to terms with the circumstances around the loss and later led to my unquenchable thirst for psychology, thanks to my largely unheralded therapist, Eduardus Ursus. He was my main source of comfort and enlightenment throughout my early childhood.

Unfortunately, he died when I was seven years old. I have remained indebted to him since, particularly for helping me overcome the effects of a period of isolation I suffered when ill as a three-year-old. Many of our conversations remain vivid to this day. Eduardus's influence during those early days led to my enduring interest and eventual work in psychotherapy.

A Teddy bear helped me cope with other childhood challenges. I will show you how and why I see him, alongside children's imaginary twins or friends, as an active talking therapist. The early part of our stroll, through the last century, presents a snapshot of the development of talking therapies in general. The later chapters will offer proof of a Teddy bear's role in those disciplines.

CHAPTER TWO

To a child, Teddy is a bridge between a human and an animal. He doesn't mind being dressed in ridiculous hats, or even being read to. You can blame him for anything, and he won't deny it. His marvellous face expresses anything a child wants to feel or hear. Peter Bull

It doesn't matter if we have been blessed with an idyllic start to life or faced deprivations, tragedies or even cruelty. What is important is how we play the hands we have been given. Attitudes and strategies used in childhood set the scene for subsequent adult behaviour. In many ways life can be viewed as a continual problem-solving exercise. That is as true for the mundane as it is for our personal, physical and mental health. Domestic decisions, marriage partner, choice of friends, career, sports and pastimes, can all be influenced by our earliest experiences. So too, are our ploys and responses in the more material world.

We can easily allow innate subconscious traits and established patterns of behaviour to determine our actions in later life.

Parents are role models. We often notice how their mannerisms appear in their offspring. 'Look at the mother', many say, 'and you'll see the prospective wife in her daughter.'

Childhood experiences can be indelible. Early exposure to music or the arts often lead to a lifetime interest in those subjects. Trauma memories can persist and eventually become the root source of phobias and prejudices. Any violence or abuse a child suffers can later be reprised onto others in adulthood.

Interaction with family and friends in a stable and secure environment is a normal part of growing up. But this can be abused if people take advantage of these trusting relationships. On a daily basis, we are all susceptible to influences such as marketing, politics, social media and peer pressure. In extreme cases of manipulation, this can lead to paedophilia or indoctrination by terrorists.

An open and pragmatic child can acquire some immunity to the possible disastrous consequences of blindly following covert impulses. Few people grow up fortunate enough in that respect to fall into the category of 'field independent' – whatever their background – where they can avoid the trap of undue influence by others in decision making. Even if we are one of the lucky ones we are still governed by Freud's maxim – *the child is father to the man* – taken from a poem (Wordsworth 1802).

CHAPTER THREE

It was an intense embrace, no awkwardness, no holding back, the kind of hug two people can only achieve after long intimacy, but anyone can give in an instant to a stuffed bear. Ada Palmer

I was three-years-old in 1942, when I was evacuated from the bombs in London to a children's home in the countryside. Whilst there, I was taken ill with gastro-enteritis. It was serious in those days It was infectious and many children succumbed to dehydration and died. I could not understand why I was separated from everybody. I hadn't been naughty and had no idea I was ill. I cannot recall any diarrhoea. I spent every day, for many months, isolated in a tiny room with a small table and chair, a rusty red Triang tricycle for exercise and a few books. I had little contact with anyone. A grumpy carer quickly dumped meals on my table and left in silence. The remainder of each day I saw nobody else until the evening.

It is well before bedtime. The nice children's nurse is here again and this time asks if I would like to go outside with her for a while. We are sitting together on the back doorstep looking over the rolling fields in the evening sunshine. I tell her I like hearing the birds singing. 'Shall we sing a song?' she asks.

We sing songs together every evening on that doorstep. I love it when she rocks and cradles me on her lap for our two favourite songs – 'You are my sunshine' and 'My bonnie lies over the ocean'. She is warm, soft and cuddly and kind. Her sweetheart is at sea in the Navy.

Today when we sing the lines 'As I lay on my pillow, I dreamt that my truelove was dead' she starts crying. She has not heard from him this week. I cuddle up to her. 'We don't want to sing that song again', I tell her.

We did though, days later, but without that verse.

She made great efforts to keep me occupied by teaching me to read and write. I cannot remember ever knowing her name. She said a tearful goodbye to me before my last few weeks at the home. She asked me to promise to *get better*. Those were definitely her farewell words but it never occurred to me then that I was ill. At the time I assumed she referred to my literacy. That – together with her genuine affection – was her most valuable contribution to my welfare. It gave me a great start to my formal education. Eventually I forgot about her and my long isolation until, cathartically, much later in life when a greater significance in our relationship emerged. In due course, I will expand upon that and in particular the songs we chose to sing.

CHAPTER FOUR

My Teddy was there when I had no friends to play with, no one to talk to, no one to share my little woes or my big joys. He looked constant and was constant. He never aged, no matter how tattered he became. His smell was the smell of my years as a boy, and he alone knew everything. Now, when I see him on the shelf, he is like my flesh and my soul – older, worn, but still full of happiness. Robert Kunciov

Back home at last.
I spot my Teddy – Big Ted. I give him a tight hug and tell him how much I missed him. It isn't really true. I feel guilty. I had forgotten him. Anyway I tell him about all the things that have happened since our long separation. I detect a smile – he's happy to see me. Maybe he'd been lonely. I know how that feels.

This developed into a long-term conversation that was sometimes oral, often telepathic, but always verbally structured rather than abstract – and imaginatively two-way. Big Ted gave me immense comfort during my early years, but one day…..

I arrive home from school, talking to myself, about the day's events. I turn to Big Ted but he's not in his usual corner. I search the room – under the bunks – everywhere. Where could I have left him? I can't remember moving him but frantically chase around the flat. He's not here. I call out to Mum.
'I can't find Ted. Where is he? He's not in the bedroom.'
'It was old and dirty and smelly,' Mum replies.

My mother had impulsively disposed of Big Ted. He was irretrievable. I was inconsolable. Mum was irredeemable. I was too upset to take issue with her. I felt even worse when my father came home.

'Why did you do that?' I hear him ask her. 'It wasn't healthy – it was filthy dirty and smelly – and he talks to it. I heard him last night when he got in from school telling it all about his day. It's not natural for a seven year-old. So it's gone off with the dustman.'

I have reflected on that event many times over the years. My mother acted out of ignorance. I didn't acknowledge, then, the stress she had been under during and after the war. She had to cope with terrifying air raids with my father working in a munitions factory or on ARP duty. She regularly had to haul shopping up eight flights of stairs to our small council flat with three young children in tow. She may have meant well, thinking she was doing the right thing, but I cannot forget the hurt. If adults can be disturbed by a child chatting to a toy, is it any wonder that so many stigmatise talking therapies?

At seven years old my loss was more to do with *attachment* than anything else. I had grown out of having long conversations with Big Ted. It was just the odd comment by then. But I was always pleased to have him around. He had shared my secrets and traumas. We were bonded by history.

Natural or not, I loved and trusted Big Ted with my entire being. True he was worn. The only fur left upon him – that I could tickle my nose with – was inside his ears and within the creases of his arms and legs. The remainder of his body was threadbare. His unique odour was both comforting and reassuring in any crisis I encountered. I would never again know the slight inclination of his head, the sly wink of an eye, the sage nod, and that benevolent smile. I even missed his frown when I had been naughty. I felt so sad thinking of him buried under tons of rubbish.

My reaction to this effrontery was a mixture of shame for acting 'childishly' and feeling an idiot for talking to a Teddy. But he was mine – not my mother's. She didn't have the right. It depressed and overwhelmed me. Feeling belittled, I was unable to vent my anger on my mother. It was after this episode that I went through a period of taking unwarranted issue with my younger siblings.

To this day I still have slight pangs of loss when I see a Teddy resembling mine. That may sound stupid and immature from an adult, but it augments my determination to guard any child's right to a relationship with an inanimate toy, a non-existent twin, an imaginary friend, or a live pet. Who can begrudge that in the turmoil of a world beset with lack of empathy and understanding and full of stupidity?

Of course, this is my recollection as a child. As an adult I have reflected on that.

CHAPTER FIVE

How many children, do you suppose, have carried a lifelong resentment of parents responsible for the surreptitious removal of their Teddy Bears? John Ziff

When writing this introductory account I discovered some new insights related to that period. One of them is a revelation.

'Eureka!' I called out to the ghost of Big Ted. It wasn't so simple – that relationship with my childhood nurse. She definitely cared for me – loved me, even – but as a child I was unaware of the reason why. It was only when revisiting that time and reflecting upon the two songs we sang that the penny dropped. The similar lyrics and structures were the key.

This is a stanza from 'You are my sunshine':

> *The other night, dear, as I lay sleeping,*
> *I dreamt I held you in my arms,*
> *When I awoke, dear, I was mistaken,*
> *So I hung my head, and I cried.*

And this, a desperate plea in every chorus:
Please don't take my sunshine away.

A similar stanza is found in 'My Bonnie lies over the ocean':

> *Last night as I lay on my pillow*
> *Last night as I lay on my bed*
> *Last night as I lay on my pillow*
> *I dreamt that my Bonnie was dead.*

This song, too, has a recurrent plea:
Bring back, bring back, bring back my Bonnie to me.

If structures alone could qualify, it could almost be claimed to be plagiarism. I was aware as a child that the young nurse directed the first song to me, and the second to her sweetheart. Both express the enormous responsibility and risks we take on when we commit to love. And both address the ever-present longing in its temporary absence and the fear of its complete loss. Her choice of songs was subconsciously influenced.

She was projecting her feelings for her sweetheart onto me in his absence. It gave her comfort. I had been as important to her as she had been to me. It was hardly my less than charming illness or my temperamental behaviour that first drew her towards me. She was genuinely concerned for my welfare. I have no doubt about that – she helped vanquish my boredom and made me happier. Why else would she have spent so much of her spare time teaching me to read and write?

I realise now that her farewell plea to me was to get better *in health* – not in studies, as I had imagined as a child. As an adult I can now see our relationship was more balanced than I thought – that pleases me.

If you have not done so, you could benefit by spending some time reviewing your own memories. In the light of adult experience, you too could find new insights and a better understanding of past events if you examine them in detail.

I do not want to indulge in autobiography. The above childhood experiences are uniquely mine — but are in other ways universal. It is hardly tragic but it had its difficult moments. You may have similar childhood memories.

This first-hand account of early experiences forms the reference point for our easy stroll along the paths of talking therapies. I realise not everyone is engrossed in psychology, and will keep what follows as simple as possible. Perhaps some of you will think it trivialises the subject. Others may not. But it will help me tie things together to show why I find Teddies and imaginary friends so important to children.

CHAPTER SIX

What is it about this inanimate object of fur and stuffing that makes it so hard to part with? As children, we were acutely aware of just how much our bears loved us, and we filled their ears with our daily doings and deepest confidences. How could one grow up and not take along this dearest of companions? Sarah McClennan

You are unlikely to have considered a Teddy bear an unsung hero. He was born around the time Freud was developing his theories. And you may have twigged that Eduardus Ursus (Latin for Edward Bear) is not the true identity of my childhood psychotherapist. It is in fact the name I presented Big Ted with 'posthumously' in honour of all children's Teddy bears, pandas, other soft toys, worry-dolls, comfort-objects and imaginary twins or friends.

He helped me discover a crucial feature behind all talking therapies. His absence made me realise how essential it was to talk about problems. His support during my experiences and crises in childhood drew me towards psychology as an adult. And I have revisited that period many times.

Subconsciously I could never forget my loss of Big Ted. I imagine it is in this respect that I exhibit all the obsessions of a devoted arctophile – someone of any age – who loves Teddies.

My young daughter's Teddy was worn into an irregular rag of about a foot square. It was still her Teddy and as validly so as any infirm beloved soul in old age. She took it everywhere with her and could not get to sleep without Teddy's smell and touch. She was much younger than I had been when she lost her Teddy – on two traumatic occasions. The first was on our return home from a holiday.

We packed the bags into the car and drove home from Heathrow. When we arrived, drowsy as she was, she insisted Teddy lie beside her in bed. He (the rag) was not in the car, the cases, or hidden in clothing. He was lost! We went through the usual procedures of last seen, where, who else saw it, until we agreed it must have been left in the pocket in front of her seat on the plane. I immediately phoned the airline. The return flight had left. But with their wonderfully genuine concern and love of children the Alitalia staff contacted the captain. He in turn had the cabin crew search our seats. (It was just like the recent quest for Shackleton, mentioned at the start). They found the scrap of faded blue rag and would return it from Italy on the first flight into Heathrow in the morning.

'This is it?' the amiable receptionist exclaimed, holding it in mid-air, attached to a large Alitalia identity tag. 'You've driven forty miles each way?,' she asked, monitoring me for other signs of insanity. 'You have no idea,' I casually replied. I left. She puzzled. Me relieved. My daughter ecstatic on my return home.

The reunion was short-lived. A few months later, whilst out shopping, Teddy was lost forever from the buggy. My daughter's grief was too much to bear. I took on the task to nullify 'forever'.

The store where Teddy came from had no more in stock. However, they did have a cute puppy from his manufacturer in exactly the same blue fur. It, too, was an expensive toy. Well, not that expensive. But you will note my natural resistance as I cut out an irregular one square foot patch of material and disposed of the pristine remainder of the *dear* chap. TLC followed. I shaved the fur until it was mostly threadbare before covering it with drizzles of Ribena, tomato ketchup, orange juice and other semi-permanent staining agents. Once washed in baby shampoo and dried and dusted with baby powder it was presented, with great trepidation, to my daughter. Smiles all round. Miraculously, Teddy was back.

It may seem that my mild obsessive-compulsive disorder (OCD) with Big Ted had somehow been transferred to my daughter. However, I reject the involvement of any Lamarckian-like theory that claims progeny can inherit parental experiences, acquired by genetic modification. Attachment to an inanimate or imaginary figure is nowadays recognised as perfectly normal in children.

(If you feel so inclined, this and the assignment of human characteristics to inanimate objects (anthropomorphism) can be explored further from the reference list at the end to early studies by Piaget, Bowlby and Vygotsky).

CHAPTER SEVEN

Having a teddy bear does not mean you are immature. They are the only ones that do not laugh when you cry. Anon

Probably you, like most people, have had personal experiences with a Teddy or 'worry-doll' or their ilk in the form of an imaginary friend. Have you ever thought why and what sustained that relationship? The answer is more complex than it may seem.

In times of crises, when stability is threatened, what could be more reassuring than finding comfort in a companion that has always been there for you, glued to your past? Teddy offers unconditional love. With him as a friend you can mull over thoughts and find solutions. Is that very different from a relationship with a professional psychotherapist?

Sadly, I lost my Teddy. His absence heightens my appreciation of his presence for others. But I could never replace him. I am totally loyal to him probably on account of the manner of his demise. I could never be a collector of other Teddies. Perhaps I still miss him. Recently I saw an old Teddy resembling him, sitting on a shelf, in a pub of all places. I was not overwhelmed with heavy clouds of grief, yet shocked at my response. It was sharp – a swift arrow that pierced my heart. From out of nowhere it left me for some minutes with a yearning for times past.

Losing Big Ted had its pros and cons. I learned to cope with loss and became more contemplative about life – more pragmatic – than I might have been. I realised at a young age how discussions with Big Ted led to openness and freedom to share opinions with others. Now, more circumspect, I talk to trusted friends on private matters without the need to chat with an inanimate Teddy anymore – that is, apart from in play.

When my kids bring the grandchildren to stay – especially around Christmas – they make for the boxes in the attic. Excitedly, they engage in make-believe conversations with the family's old soft toys and revive old memories for their parents. I am delighted to join in those dialogues.

Many child therapists have acknowledged the role a Teddy bear plays in childhood. Donald Winnicott spoke of *objective reality*. He, as well as Melanie Klein and Anna Freud, regularly referred to Sigmund Freud's description of it as a *transitional object* acting as a replacement for the mother.

They furthermore cited the forced separation of a child with its Teddy as cruelty. In my case it was pure ignorance – but still painful.

Omitted from those commentaries – apart from encouraging children to express themselves privately – is the idea that Teddy bears can play another more active role. They share something that appears in all forms of psychotherapy.

Really? In *all* talking therapies, you ask? I will explain.

CHAPTER EIGHT

An experienced Teddy Bear brings with him a lifetime of knowledge and experience; the wisdom of silence and the stillness in moments of great turmoil. The long-suffering patience that is learned when belonging to a child who coming of age and coping with the bewilderment that this period of time can bring, is what he does best. The experienced bear has seen life through the heart and eyes of a child grown to adulthood and perhaps even accompanied that adult all the way to the end of the road.
Ted Menton

Talking therapies can, unquestionably, be effective. Professionally, unfortunately, they can be restricted. A lack of funding, too few therapists and the expense of private treatment – or scepticism or denial – often places psychotherapy out of reach for many people. Long waiting lists for treatment in the NHS do little to alleviate this. Stigmatisation can still present a hurdle for people to overcome before seeking professional help.

Some may simply talk to a friend about problems and find that useful. Why is that? How can an untrained ear help dampen or extinguish anxieties? Within 'just talking' something must be hidden. That same something is concealed in all forms of psychotherapy – be it deeply structured or generic counselling.

Can anything be covertly shared across a spectrum that ranges from the many forms of intense psychoanalysis right through to the simpler cognitive approaches of modern therapies? Or just talking to a trusted listener? *Or a Teddy bear?*

It does exist. It is simple. It plays a significant role in unravelling distress and resolving problems. In essence, all psychotherapies come under the category of 'talking cures', but that is only a clue to the connection.

A Teddy bear can be a genuine therapist. His input is as valid as any recognised practitioner. He shares a *modus operandi* with all therapists. Children see him as a good listener, exuding unconditional love, support, trust and confidentiality. He is also non-confrontational. The hidden feature that operates within both recognised disciplines and with Teddies might surprise you.

Entrenched psychoanalysts may judge modern simpler treatments, such as cognitive behavioural therapy, as remote from their fields. Hardened CBT practitioners often dismiss analytical in-depth investigation as superfluous, slow and uneconomic. Both probably have practitioners who view Teddy bears as light years away from their work. I say they are wrong. All are related.

A child engages naturally with a Teddy bear. Such trust and openness is important in 'talking cures'. Since Freud's days we have seen many therapies develop over the past century. They range from complex to simple. Some evolve from practitioners' experience – some from new theories and psychological enquiry. Talking therapies are always in flux – their popularities alter and they come in and out of fashion. But the appeal of a

Teddy bear has steadily broadened over those years. It began simply as a cuddly toy. Today its role is wider and more active.

CHAPTER NINE

There's just something about a Teddy bear that's impossible to explain. When you hold one in your arms, you get a feeling of love, comfort and security. It's almost supernatural. James Ownby

Teddy bears first appeared in 1903, independently in two countries – America and Germany. Limited and extremely slow international communication in those days supports the view that their creators were unaware of each other – yet another example of synchronicity in the history of mankind.

The American toy has a Presidential provenance. One day, Theodore (Teddy) Roosevelt was shocked to witness bear hunters tormenting and severely injuring a cub. He put a stop to it, and had the animal humanely put out of its agony. The story got out to the press and the President was lampooned in a cartoon of the incident. His political opponents took the opportunity to demean and chide him using his nickname and naming the dead cub Teddy's bear. An empathic public supported his action.

Toy manufacturer Morris Michtom spotted the commercial value of this story, and began producing soft cuddly versions of the animal. He petitioned

President Roosevelt and gained permission to use his nickname to market the toy as a Teddy bear. It was a runaway success and earned Michtom a fortune.

Also in 1903, in Germany – with no evidence of any connection to events in America – the Steiff company launched its newest toy. This bear was not as soft and cuddly as Michtom's. It boasted a more structured Teutonic figure. These were made to last. Despite the attentions of their young owners, many survive to this day. The original Steiff bears (identifiable by a button in their ear) are valuable treasures sought after by specialist collectors.

Since its inception the Teddy bear has been unassailably popular both with children and adults. It inspired the two-step 'The Teddy Bears' Picnic'. Special events are put on these days for children *and their parents* to share with their Teddy bears. Have you ever attended a Teddy bear concert? I took my youngsters to one at the Barbican in London. Sheer joy! The exhilaration of hundreds of children and adults introducing their Teddies to a mixture of classical and popular music was pure transcendental magic when they all joined in to sing;

If you go down in the woods today
You're sure of a big surprise
If you go down in the woods today
You'd better go in disguise!
For every bear that ever there was
Will gather there for certain
Because today's the day the
Teddy Bears have their picnic
Picnic time for Teddy Bears
The little Teddy Bears are having

TEDDY BEAR AND FREUD

A lovely time today

Watch them, catch them unawares

And see them picnic on their holiday

See them gaily gad about

They love to play and shout

They never have any cares

At six o'clock their Mommies and Daddies

Will take them home to bed

Because they're tired little Teddy Bears

Recently, quite by accident, I came across a group of toddlers having a picnic with their Teddy bears in a wood. Their primary school used the occasion as an educational tool to introduce them to nature studies.

More formal – and often commercial – Teddy bear events abound, like the one at The Swiss Garden in Shuttleworth, Bedfordshire, where families go to treat their Teddies to fun and games along with – of course – a picnic.

Teddy bears are entrenched in our psyche. Their popularity is evident in the many characters familiar to all of us –Paddington with his quirky wisdom, Sooty, Yogi and Boo Boo, Rupert Bear. The list goes on. Aloysius (Sebastian's bear) plays a major role in Evelyn Waugh's *Brideshead Revisited*. Pudsey takes centre stage, raising funds for the *Children in Need* charity. A Panda is the representative for the *Wild Life Fund*. Baloo bear is Mowgli's tutor in Rudyard Kipling's *The Jungle Book*. The names seem unending.

Until the film *Goodbye Christopher Robin* was released, few people knew that Winnie the Pooh was a real bear that lived in London Zoo. He (she in real life) became the pet of A.A Milne's son Christopher Robin before the author's children's stories brought him to life for the masses.

A. A. Milne's book introduced the world to Winnie in 1926.

"You can't be in London for a long time without going to the Zoo. There are some people who begin the Zoo at the beginning, called WAYIN, and walk as quickly as they can past every cage until they get to the one called WAYOUT, but the nicest people go straight to the animal they love the most and stay there. So when Christopher Robin goes to the Zoo, he goes to where the polar bears are, and he whispers something to the third keeper from the left, and doors are unlocked, and we wander through dark passages and up steep stairs, until at last we come to the special cage, and the cage is opened, and out trots something brown and furry, and with a happy cry of 'Oh, Bear!' Christopher Robin rushes into its arms. Now this bear's name is Winnie, which shows what a good name for bears it is, but the funny thing is we cannot remember whether Winnie is called after Pooh, or Pooh after Winnie. We did know once, but we have forgotten...."

(You can find a biography of the real Winnie in chapter twenty-five).

CHAPTER TEN

Age simply doesn't enter into it! The older the friend, the more he is valued, particularly when he shows so visibly the characteristics that we all look for in friends. You have only to look at a genuine teddy's face to see at once the loyalty, common sense, and above all, dependability behind it. Peter Bull

You now know a little more about a Teddy, but not yet about his importance as Eduardus Ursus, the psychotherapist.

As adults we could see Teddy bears in that role more easily, if we regressed a little to childhood. It's difficult to achieve that innocence. Ewan McGregor attempted it in the film *Christopher Robin*. You, too, could give it a try.

As a child I was aware that verbalisation helped solve problems. I came to realise that, when chatting to Big Ted about isolation and my nurse. I could not confidently confide in anybody – except him. That was okay with me. Even if I knew it was make-believe when he responded, I accepted his imaginary nods or frowns or laughter.

Did you ever watch *Mr Bean* convey thoughts to his audience by conversing with his Teddy in his TV series? Most people would be inhibited to copy him. But, encouraged to do so, some can benefit from it as a treatment.

In Teddy bear therapy, adults under stress reconnect with underlying memories triggered by their bear. They address him by name and keep him at hand at all times including the workplace (with an explanation if necessary), and at night in bed. The soft cuddly toy can evoke associated childhood experiences to compensate for past lack of affection and attention. If it's a new bear it can still help address current low self-esteem, suppressed anger, or shyness. When difficult events are recalled, by speech or thought, with a Teddy it can help trace causal features behind them. With an old Teddy, its smell or touch can readily turn thoughts to the past. That focus, with adult interpretation, can promote reflection and reconstruction.

All talking cures elicit words that describe abstractions, release feelings, and eventually create structure for suppressed or traumatic events. These new words become signposts to objectivity. Attempts to verbally communicate nebulous ideas and emotions – *to others* – necessarily require words. These, in effect, become labels for description and clarification. The new labels help yield a more accurate view of reality (which is never in fact definitive – we all have different commentaries for identical events). Does this process operate with a Teddy bear?

Prosperity Place (see reference page) gave an example of a distressed adult's experience with a Teddy from which I quote:

'I had a strong urge to buy a teddy bear. I found one that was warm and cuddly. I felt weepy and sad, so I got into bed and curled up with the teddy bear.

I started crying and found myself talking out loud about my feelings. I felt as if I was a young child who was hurt and wounded. Suddenly, I had a strong image in my mind of myself when I was three years old. I was standing by my baby brother's crib feeling alone and left out.

Tears came for what seemed like a long time. I knew the pain I was releasing was very deep. When it was over, I felt as if I had released the weight of years of pain, and I realized how strong an effect the birth of my brother had had on me. The effect of the experience with the teddy bear was extremely healing. The bear enabled me to reach back in time to touch unreleased emotions that were stored deep inside of me — emotions that needed to be released in order for me to heal.'

In the same source, Joan Sotkin, on July 16th, 2002, offered a succinct account of Teddy bear therapy. Here are a few extracts:

'First, find yourself a teddy bear that feels good to hold. Give your teddy bear a name. Make it a real companion that you can talk to and confide in. Yes, you may feel silly doing this at first, but no one is going to know about it except you

When you feel uncomfortable or unhappy, tell the teddy bear how you feel. Talk out loud. Use the phrase I feel _____.

Any time you are feeling sad or uncomfortable, lie down and cuddle up with your teddy bear. Say, out loud, I feel so uncomfortable. Try to define the feeling. (I feel sad, I feel angry, I feel alone, etc.) This is an effective release technique

Releasing feelings is often difficult and takes practice, especially if you were not allowed to express your feelings as a child. '

In *American Thinker*, (see reference page), Richard F. Miniter wrote an article *'Teddy Bear Therapy Versus the Mental Health Professionals'*.

I picked out a few lines:

'Teddy Bears have done more for children than every child psychologist, child therapist, children's support group or parenting "expert" who ever opened a case file. So why do we keep listening to these people?'

'In large part it's because parents are reluctant to believe that "normal" behavior or physicality in children extends over such a broad range. That it includes children reading at either two or ten. It includes late-talkers and early bloomers, emotionally strong and the emotional. In short that children aren't identical hothouse roses but instead a bouquet of variegated wildflowers.'

'Above all think twice and thrice before you hand over your child's feelings and self-impression over to "professionals" to manage for you at $150 an hour. So maybe more confidently, and certainly in more joy, you can go the Teddy Bear route instead.'

I do not share that general view of 'professionals', but do see Teddy bears as the most widely used and the least acknowledged therapists of all time.

Big Ted – acting as *my therapist* Eduardus Ursus – left a deep indebtedness upon me. He certainly helped replicate the love and support I missed from the nurse at my sick room. I mulled over those difficult early experiences with him. It helped me develop some insight and a more accurate narrative of those events. Indeed, this champion of psychotherapy was an enduring influence on my work in psychology.

CHAPTER ELEVEN

Long before I grew up, my Teddy bear taught me what love really meant: being there when you're needed. Jim Nelson

You might dismiss my claims for a Teddy bear as fanciful. Carl Rogers, a respected therapist in the 1950s, with a basically unresponsive, non-interventional, non-judgemental style, hardly differed in his approach. At the very least, talking to a Teddy offers a path away from childhood egocentricity – with its focus only on self. That imaginary dialogue can highlight to the child how its own behaviour affects another person. Such regular conversations in our younger years can continue into adulthood. Many people express themselves in diaries and personal journals. Putting thoughts into a diary is now superseded by *conversations* with new technological gadgets like *Replika, Echo, Alexa, Eliza* and similar chatbots. No doubt, one day, robots will be in the forefront of new forms of psychotherapy. When they are, they may resolve the shortage of practitioners. I digress – more on that subject later.

The importance of Teddies to children's welfare has been widely recognised across society. Perhaps surprisingly, is an example reported in a constabulary by The Dundee Evening Telegraph May 17th 2018:

'Police in Dundee have been "truly and utterly humbled" by the number of Trauma Teddies handed in to officers ahead of the launch of the comforting scheme. The initiative will see hand-knitted teddy bears handed out to young children involved in traumatic incidents within the local area, such as car crashes, in a bid to comfort them.

Despite not officially being rolled out, a teddy has already been issued to a young child involved in a collision in the city last week. The force previously appealed to members of the public to send in their own knitted teddies and have revealed they've received creations from as far afield as England and Shetland.

Inspector Chris Boath, Longhaugh Locality inspector, was delighted at the number of Trauma Teddies sent in. He said: "We have been stunned by the response we have received from the knitters of the area, and can only ask you to please keep them coming, we can never have enough of them.

"Such has been the response, that in conjunction with Children 1st, we are creating 'Starter Packs' for distribution across the country to other community teams who have expressed an interest in running schemes of their own. "Thank you again to everyone who has contributed, for your generosity and your time."

Teddy talk can be compared to similar conversations in the Confessional with a priest; talking to the deceased; talking to pets; talking to inanimate objects; talking to an imaginary twin or friend; talking out loud to oneself (Hamlet's soliloquy – to be or not…) or talking internally to self – the inner ongoing dialogue we all indulge in at times.

I had an eclectic approach with clients and engaged in a range of disciplines, suited to each individual. I came to the conclusion that a Teddy bear has something in common with ALL those forms of therapy.

Before I can expect you to concur with that finding I may need to summarise the main therapies for you. Consider what follows as a brief primer to set them side-by-side and bring that one common denominator into view.

Psychotherapy is a broad subject. Its spectrum covers profound analyses as well as the simpler behavioural ones and general counselling, including occupational formats. You may already be familiar with them. I have placed various related disciplines in clusters and without examination in depth. If so inclined, you can find more detailed descriptions readily from reference books or via the Internet. It is not necessary to do so here to show the intrinsic relationship between these clusters.

No specific expertise or knowledge in any of these fields is required to recognise the hidden key element common to all such therapies.

CHAPTER TWELVE

The world of the teddy bear is an innocent one, a world that gives delight and hurts not, a world that appeals to all generations and all nationalities. Gyles Brandreth

If you prefer, feel free to quickly scan the associated narratives that follow. They essentially show how much they have in common with Teddy bears.

Should you require hard proof you can find it in the appendix with a range of therapies examined in tabular form for easy comparison.

The father of psychotherapy was – arguably – Sigmund Freud. He proposed an intuitive theory that – although non-empirical (i.e. without hard data) and therefore unscientific – became the basis for all further studies of the human mind. After 100 years he remains in the public eye to this day – aligned to our subconscious thoughts and motives – forever associated with psychology.

Current practitioners of psychotherapy, even if not Freudian adherents, will still seek deeper reasons for behaviour and cannot ignore subconscious drives behind actions. At the very least Freud's ideas of the ego, super-ego and id, have spawned many other forms of therapy over the last century.

Carl Jung and Alfred Adler and others proposed similar non-scientific theories to develop their techniques.

Jungian psychoanalysts treat their clients with mediation similar to Freud but focussed upon other theoretical subconscious features. Here once more, after establishing new patterns of thinking, the therapist embarks on the search for possible subconscious roots behind actions. Long conversations and exchanges of ideas, often over months or years, are required to label thoughts and identify abstractions to produce objective structures to help resolve entrenched issues.

Adler's theory promoted the notion that an inferiority complex was at the crux of psychological upsets. Once more the subconscious mind was seen in turmoil.

These deeply analytical approaches form our first cluster. Unquestionably they are 'talking therapies'. The analysand (person undergoing analysis) offers inner thoughts for detailed analysis at great length and expense.

Generally the analyst is the smaller voice in the dialogue and is non-directive. For people who can afford the time and expense such analyses can be fruitful. Often analysis is initiated by current problems. Other reasons vary. It could be curiosity, self-indulgence, or as part of training in therapy.

As it progresses, analysis helps heighten self-awareness and promotes a template to deal with new crises. Unearthed abstractions – such as feelings and events from the past – are scrutinised in detail. Their influence is considered crucial in mental life. The analyst's goal is to help identify those factors and expose how they affect the client's thoughts and behaviour.

Structures offered here are stepping stones that help mediate the abstract with reality. Whether Freudian, or the more symbolic and transcendental Jungian or the inferiority complex of the Adlerian theory, its success is mainly due to its covert link to all other therapies – shared too, *with Teddy bears*.

Much of the material examined in this type of 'talking cure' is generated by long forgotten or vivid traumas from childhood. Sometimes they can only be described in a sentient form. Dominant smells, tastes, sounds or visual images, can both impair or help the resolution of painful memories. I have always taken an open approach in practice and have rented psychoanalysis on a short lease for several clients. Occasionally that was the key to success.

I offer some simplified examples of such interventions for illustration here and later on. (Fuller, fictionalised, accounts appear in my novel *A Bird Stuck on the Sky*).

Liam terrified his wife with bizarre reactions to random events. Several psychiatrists had labelled him with a personality disorder – and could find no answer to his problem. Immediately I met him I sensed a deeply subconscious motor at work. When questioned about his behaviour, his quiet demeanour quickly turned to anger. Behind that response was intense fear. We looked at several diverse episodes in turn.

Things were brought to a head when his wife put on a new dress and he ripped it off her without any explanation. In previous examples of irrationality he had stormed out of a holiday hotel and refused to enter a theatre to enjoy a long-booked show. He had a history of similar incidents and more minor unexplained behaviour.

Talking calmly, to begin with, he gradually became more agitated as he related details that preceded his weird reactions. Panic ensued in each case as he faced his ordeals. With gentle coaxing he identified the cause of his terror. It was a colour. Eventually he was able to name it and for the very first time he spluttered out the word – purple. The dress he tore off his wife's back; the décor of the hotel room he rejected; the curtains in a theatre foyer he could not enter; all were a deep purple hue. It hid a fearful trauma – so strong that it was forced into repression. This abstractive colour had created a covert phobia. It had to be addressed. Its source was eventually located, deeply embedded in his sub-conscious from childhood. Still a toddler, Liam had been separated from his brother after their mother died. They had barely kept in touch since. On renewing their acquaintance, the elder sibling recalled their mother's funeral. Liam last saw her shrouded in purple.

Jennifer was suffering from bouts of anxiety. She had some minor domestic issues with her marriage. The local vicar was a comfort and acted as her counsellor. They became close friends, sharing an interest in reading. She reported a recurring nightmare that sent her flying off to the Isle of Man.

Taking the Freudian view that dreams of flying have a sexual origin, and with little else to go on, I focussed on her dream. It mirrored her real life predicament. But she needed to find and experience the answer first hand. I had her repeat the phrase 'Isle of Man' over and over until its phonetics lost all meaning. In due course it segued into 'I love man' – a covert reference to the vicar. She loved her husband not him. The dream alerted her to the suppressed hidden danger recognised by her sub-conscious mind. Neither she, nor the vicar, was aware of transference (which can result in a crush on the therapist). She approached her husband who helped resolve the missing elements in their marriage.

It is clear to me that psychoanalytical therapies can be effective. In an attenuated form they are as valid as any other talking therapy. One could question the benefits of full analyses. Certainly, diminishing returns on years of effort and ever-increasing expense put such trials out of reach for most people. The rich vein of rewards from short forays into that world can be economic and relatively easy pickings.

The analytical approach may seem profound – too intellectual for some, perhaps. However it can readily formulate unexpressed notions into structures that help bridge the subconscious with reality.

Surprisingly it owes much of its successful outcomes to a single hidden factor shared with and exploited by Eduardus Ursus and other Teddy bears.

I will introduce you to that covert component after we examine other forms of talking therapy during our stroll, hand in hand with Freud and a Teddy bear, from the early days of the past century.

CHAPTER THIRTEEN

A bear knows all your secrets – and keeps them. Rosanne Brown

More structured processes appeared in the wake of the heavyweight psychoanalyses. This particular cluster includes Gestalt and other insight-directed therapies along with transactional formats and other construct theories. They differ from their antecedents in several ways. In practice they are simpler with far shorter courses. They are usually tutorial – insight-directed – as opposed to the generally non-interventionist approach of psychoanalysis. Certainly they have a place at the table, being economic in both cost and time – and effective.

Fritz and Laura Perls developed Gestalt therapy. The essence of their theory is that 'the whole adds up to more than the sum of the parts'. They considered that a combination of tiny, apparently trivial, factors are behind chaos and general unhappiness.

A good analogy can be found in music, where separate notes can form chords. Chords, in essence, are gestalts. They project greater harmony than the notes played singly.

That reminds me of Jimmy (Schnozzle) Durante singing, '*The Guy who found the Lost Chord*'. Sitting at his piano, he faced the same difficulties – as encountered by Gestalt therapists sitting with patients – when trying to make salient connections.

Here are a few extracts from his lyrics:

> *You know it wasn't easy finding the lost chord.*
> *First I put an A flat with a B minor,*
> *Then I put a B minor with an F major,*
> *Then I put an F minor with a B major,*
> *Then I tried an A and a B and a B and a C,*
> *And a C and a D and a D and E and an E and an F,*
> *And an F and a G.........*

Finally, on discovering the blend, the song ends with:

> *So let's celebrate. I'm feeling great,*
> *I'm the guy that found the lost chord.*

And he radiates the same elation that anybody, therapist or not, will recognise on solving a testing puzzle. Gestalt therapists sift through seemingly minor incidents in patients' accounts – in place of musical notes – in their search for congruity.

Harry ran a garage with his brother, he in charge of servicing, the brother on sales. The brother was taken seriously ill. Harry had to take over demonstrating cars, but his long-held fear of driving too far – particularly on motorways – came to the fore. In the course of a couple of sessions I learned about two important past triggers. His mother abruptly left the family when he was little. And, one day he returned home from school as a latchkey child to find the house on fire.

Harry had given no further thought to either event since childhood. He accepted these lightly repressed episodes from his younger days as the root of his problem. It was one of the shortest analyses I ever made. Its insight and a behavioural desensitisation programme cured his phobia. When free of his fear a new gestalt gelled. Harry realised how much he missed his mother, estranged since childhood. He traced her and renewed their relationship to their mutual joy.

Transactional Analysis (TA) is another format within this cluster. Created by Eric Berne and championed in his widely popularised book *Games People Play*, we are presented with a Parent/Child/Adult triad that operates within individuals.

TA aims to alter long held childish thoughts and emotions into adult responses and constructs and a more objective viewpoint. It may well be mimicked as an active component in a child's dialogue with a Teddy bear. In much the same way as therapist-led TA can help resolve internalised conflicts, a child can project ideas to and fro with a Teddy bear. Innocent contemplation within a TA-like triad could help transform the child's self-criticism and rebelliousness towards more mature behaviour and acceptance. Chats with Big Ted certainly taught me to dampen my internal 'rebellious child' (Berne's term) during conflicts with my mother and others.

On one occasion I utilised TA to treat a petulant young lady after arranging to see her entire family. The daughter arrived first with her boyfriend. He had been hanging around outside, waiting for her. Her behaviour was evident from the outset. The lad meekly asked why she was late. She remained quiet. He became annoyed. 'Don't you have a go at me,' she said and glanced around for sympathy. I had anticipated several long sessions, but her body language presented a crucial clue. The young lady slightly, but consistently, flicked her head to one side, even to clearly neutral questions from other sources. It was a marker of subtle aggression, indicating her 'rebellious child' within.

The family offered their accounts and were invited to play each other's roles. The father regularly lost his temper and threatened to slap his daughter's face. The rest of the family had ignored her tic-like head movements. She was regularly flinching at them. Nobody had copied it when playing her role. They pointedly added it to their repertoire – which angered her.
'You're not aware you're doing it?' 'No, I suppose it's just me being nervous,' she said.

Unconsciously employed to get her own way, her victimising flinch made people feel angry, then sorry and guilty. Her father had been hoodwinked. It triggered his further threats or uncontrolled slaps. 'Chicken and egg' – he felt obliged to make amends after losing his temper. Any neutral observation was met with the same petulance and required some effort even on my part not to be intimidated by responding to the accusative twitch. With the key source of their arguments exposed, the family screened the daughter's behaviour and she actively avoided flinching. Their relationships improved and counselling came to a fruitful end.

Moving on from TA, the inestimable value of Aaron Beck's work with Cognitive Behavioural Therapy is now fully recognised as an effective and economic talking cure. It revolves around thinking and defining exactly how we feel in situations. Whilst past experiences are not excluded, the focus here is mainly on current behaviour. Once again the inevitable labelling that arises, when using descriptive words, leads to structured thinking with its inherent signposts to objectivity. To some extent Harry's problems were loosely analysed in this manner. Some cases are clearly resolved with CBT.

A lady terrified of spiders failed to respond to a standard desensitisation programme. Her reactions became so severe that she checked into a hotel for a day if a spider appeared at home. Unaligned to that she became unduly anxious if her husband was late getting home. She expressed her fear of being alone at home – but with no reference to spiders. Her long-standing milder phobia of spiders had become acute over the course of the past year or two. Why? A short analysis revealed a connection between the spouse and the spider – an association with the fear of death. Her husband was her senior by many years. They were both ageing. She repressed the thought of him dying and leaving her alone by projecting her angst onto her phobia. She soon faced up to her situation. With the cause of her anxieties resolved, she responded well to behavioural therapy. So well in fact, that she learned to hold a spider in her hand and tolerate any tardiness in her husband.

No doubt several of the other methods mentioned could have helped resolve the 'spider lady's' relationship. They, too, could have given insight into Jennifer's dilemma.

It's strange, isn't it, that so many different theories revolve around three elements? Freudians use ego, super-ego and id; Adlerians, inferiority complex/ideal self/ real self; Jungian's, ego/personal unconscious/ancestral unconscious. Perhaps this can be seen as evidence of Jung's existential synchronicity. But I digress once more.

'Mindfulness' is currently in vogue and has its roots in Buddhism and meditation. It challenges and ushers people away from ruminating over the past. The idea here is to live in the moment. This can be aided by drawing attention to the minutiae in everyday living. Attention to breathing patterns, concentration on details during eating, or how one walks can promote unity between thoughts and actions. Non-judgemental observations such as these can help people detach themselves from automatic thoughts and reactions learned in the past. Once these past patterns have been interrupted new words are employed to describe current behaviour. New words are new labels. Labels create new structures. Structured thinking leads to objectivity.

Mindfulness can help resolve everyday stresses or more recent or 'surface' problems in life. But I do have some reservations. Dangers can arise if deeper issues involving the subconscious are causal factors. The persistent use of mindfulness in these circumstances could lead to profounder long-term suppressions.

I faced a parallel effect with a desperate patient who had been on antidepressants for about a decade. They were prescribed directly after her husband had suddenly died after thirty or so years in a happy marriage. Her new GP agreed that I could try counselling her while she slowly withdrew from her medication. Some weeks later she began going through the recognised stages of bereavement. 'It was as if he had died last week', she said. The mourning process thawed as fresh as the day it was, when originally suppressed – by her medication – into the deep freeze of her subconscious.

Counselling helped her identify the source of her depression. When completed, she no longer required any more antidepressants. Perhaps, if she had owned a cherished Teddy bear at the time of her husband's death – with cuddles and 'chats' – she might have grieved naturally and avoided medication and its damaging side-effects.

The senses – particularly smell – can harbour deeply subconscious memories. So, too, can responses to art and music. Both feature in my penultimate cluster where remedial therapies apply these stimuli. Rather like psychoanalysis the focus here is to expose the subconscious or other motors behind overt behaviour.

The quest for new objectivity taking a route mediated by art or music can provide an appropriate bridge. Hidden thoughts and entrenched feelings, or novel responses expressed in abstracted forms, can then be identified and labelled. Active creation of free art forms can describe a host of motives, reactions and emotions. Therapists can then offer suggestions to help label these representations with words.

Youngsters who have suffered severe traumas may present themselves as 'elective mutes'. Recent evidence suggests this is not always wilful on the child's part. Language skills can be blocked neurologically. This can manifest as losses in previously utilised lexicons and structural language. Whatever the reason, whether transient or resilient, the loss of competence has to be addressed. In guiding towards the re-acquisition and re-establishment of language, gentle reinforcement of residual components can be useful. Resurrected abstractions help re-develop that learning process.

People – particularly children – can be encouraged to express their inner thoughts and fears in art form to close that gap.

Therapist, Lauren Fox-McLoughlan explains:

'Art psychotherapy functions in a variety of ways, depending on the client and their needs. The image (a term which here refers to both 2 and 3D creations) becomes a third person in the room, so the therapeutic dyad becomes a triad – the work is not just between the therapist and the client, but between the therapist, client and image. The image can serve to embody the intense feelings that cannot be verbalised, as well as potentially diluting the self-consciousness that the intensity of one-to-one therapy can create, allowing feelings to emerge and be expressed without shame or embarrassment. The creative process and resulting tangible images that exist in the world outside of one's head can be helpful to map therapeutic work and progress over time, especially when someone's personal narrative has been disrupted by trauma and a linear thread through time is hard to find.

When Paula came to art psychotherapy as an adult, there was a traumatic event in her past she was struggling to directly address. The words would not come, and it was as if her conscious mind was protecting her from what happened by refusing to let her focus on and process what happened verbally. Paula explored various art materials, often as a distraction from the intensity of being in close proximity to another in one-to-one therapy. After several sessions, when our therapeutic relationship had been established, Paula used the art materials to make an image of what she was so frightened of speaking directly about. This image was very powerful to her, and something that embodied the strong feelings she had about the event. Because she had externalised some of her feelings around the trauma into an image on paper, she had something tangible which we could begin to get closer to together. She had a physical object she could turn away from when she needed to, and was able to *physically measure her distance from the image based on what she was able to manage. She could turn the image over, or put it away when she began to feel overwhelmed, and we were able to broach the event in bite size or manageable chunks.'*

That account emphasises the mediation process that operates in most forms of psychotherapy where it is imperative to search for abstractions and deeply buried subconscious thoughts operating behind distress. When identified with words they can help create structure leading to objectivity and a clearer view of reality.

'Music has charms to soothe the savage breast' **William Congreve (1697)**
Music therapists mediate by discussing the tone, tempo, and arrangement of musical compositions and their emotional impact on mood, memories, motivation, etc. When labelled in this manner objective structure can be placed on occult ideas. One feature that cannot be overlooked is the purely physical effect that music has on our senses. When music produces strong subconscious and spontaneous visceral effects, it can be therapeutic. Various pitches and rhythms can profoundly affect our bodies' responses and release tears, raise hairs on the back of necks, modulate breathing and heartbeat and stimulate feelings connected to forgotten important or traumatic events.

Shumini Suzuki was clearly aware of that when he developed his unique approach for teaching to play the violin for young children. He employed loose, non-structured lessons that appealed to their innate senses. In many instances the violin becomes a transitional object with its accompanied attachment for the child.

Professor Nigel Osborne, in his clinic in Mostar, used music to treat people suffering from post-traumatic stress disorder (PTSD) from the Bosnian war.

He also developed a unique form of psychotherapy with his Rock School of Music to help bond and reconcile Croats and Bosnians after their Civil War.

Music is strongly related to mathematics in structure. Mathematicians use symbols to identify and solve theoretical equations. Similarly scores can be analysed as balancing sounds into resolution. Such a balance can be mimicked alongside associated personal problems. Disharmony in music – dissonance psychologically – can be emotionally disturbing. Composers intend that effect on occasion. But disquiet, brought on by music with historical associations for people, is a different matter. Here therapy commences. Music can trigger overt responses that act as mediators to help unravel subconscious material behind behaviour.

Newly employed away from home, a young Scottish lady became increasingly unhappy living in England. With a strong attachment to Scotland she had arrived with her set of bagpipes. Unfortunately whenever she played them they induced more distress. We discussed a possible reunion of the instrument and its musical home. It chimed with her deep yearning. She decided to take the pipes with her for a break up in Scotland. Sitting alone, in the centre of the vast expanse of Glencoe, she spent an entire day playing her pipes – often in tears – as they triggered long-forgotten thoughts and traumas. It must have been a truly wonderful scenario to witness. The catharsis was quite extraordinary; she found herself, and returned to England a contented soul.

Many distressed people have found help and solace from the Mind organisation, the Samaritans, Alcoholics Anonymous, gambling and drug addiction help-lines, religious interventionists, and various other groups. All aim at relieving distress and changing behaviour. They can help people join support groups or live within certain limited parameters. The influence of the group or the restrictions of a regime can establish a more constructive lifestyle. When maintained, this can compete with and control destructive thoughts or actions. But without new labelling, objectivity is not so easily achieved within these groups. Primarily this type of counselling is supportive. As a rule, clients are directed to other talking therapies when needed. Individual counselling is limited by skill-sets, workloads and other logistics. The dedicated people, often volunteers, working in these fields make a very important contribution to society, which is why I include them within this final cluster.

And lastly, religion has its place for many people. Whether a believer or not, for the moment disregard Mark Twain with his Pudd'nhead Wilson's description of faith as, *'believing what you know ain't so'*. Possibly the verbalisation element within the Confessional with a Roman Catholic priest can bring solace and solutions to some people. Does praying or talking to the imaginary differ widely from talking to a Teddy bear?

CHAPTER FOURTEEN

In a world gone bad, a bear - even a bear standing on its head - is a comforting, uncomplicated, dependable hunk of sanity. Pam Brown

Let's reflect on the therapies outlined in previous chapters and compare them.

Did you notice any features common to all of them, *including a child and a Teddy*?

Can there possibly be any unifying factor for such a wide range of treatments?

Could a child's comfort from a Teddy bear and the full gamut of therapies from deep psychoanalysis to simpler behavioural therapies share such a unique feature?

The answer is yes. It lies partly in what is known as psycholinguistics – the connection between language and psychology. It is not essential here, but detailed studies of this subject can be referenced from exponents such as Noam Chomsky and Lev Vygotsky, who claimed *'language is the tool of tools'*.

We do not need to examine the learning process for language (heuristics) in any depth. The acquisition of language is a universal early developmental stage in all human beings, whatever their culture. Words are used initially to identify objects, then to communicate and conceptualise ideas to others and to self. Individual words help categorise these ideas and maintain memory banks.

The more specific the word is, the more accurate any concept can be disseminated, discussed or retrieved from memory. For example, if we describe two closely similar colours in terms of one single colour they become difficult to relate to conceptually. 'Darker' or 'lighter' has far less accuracy than the distinction between violet and blue.

We naturally use words to act as symbols to describe physical forms and overt actions in our everyday intercourse. We do not have to do so to experience emotions and abstract ideas, or to appreciate music or art. We can carry out routine-learned tasks with simple imagery. But if we want to convey those responses to others we need to use appropriate language.

When we face personal problems in life how do we solve them? Usually we find solutions with an inner dialogue to label and clarify the components involved.

If we lack the ability to do that, we are stymied.

In childhood we lack experience and have a limited vocabulary. A toddler cannot accurately assign words to feelings. It can be impossible, in those early years, to organise thoughts for any realistic reflection or transmission to others. Infants, unable to find suitable words, cannot categorise and store memories for easy retrieval. With sparse access to verbal descriptions they cannot resolve childhood concerns or traumas. The natural response, when stressed by this impasse, is to seek unconditional comfort with warm cuddles and empathy. That is often from maternal or paternal sources but can be provided by siblings or family pets or inanimate toys – and in particular Teddy bears.

When a child turns to a Teddy bear it acts as a substitute for living alternatives. As a relationship develops it becomes the transitional object (Winnicott, 1952) where the child can share thoughts and emotions. These cannot be labelled without words. However the smell and physical attributes of the toy are reassuring and easily bonded to experiences and feelings.

Once the child begins to acquire language it will increasingly be used to converse with Teddy in thought and overt speech. This dialogue can be a crucial factor in the child's formative years.

In stressful circumstances a Teddy bear can act as a locum psychotherapist. The trio elements of labels, objectivity and structure readily apply here as in all the recognised forms of therapy. And this one single component common to all is deeply buried but easily excavated. It is intrinsic to language.

When we have to describe abstract ideas we have no alternative, other than to use words as labels. The one obvious exception is music, where accurate notes and annotations in a score are definitive in a fashion unmatched by words. Many argue that music could be the most complex and the most accurate of all human communication.

With words as labels we can review entrenched emotions and unchain suppressed thoughts. Objective structures for memories help us reflect and re-organise our reality. Deep psychoanalysis may give a fuller comprehension of self *vis-à-vis* the external world, but in essence it is based upon re-labelling experiences. Freud, et al, used the intermediary of the subconscious. TA and Gestalt targeting ploys help re-name behaviour. Almost every form of talking therapy does exactly that.

Can you possibly imagine thinking about a new task without an ongoing internal conversation? If we are preparing food don't we speak to ourselves as we go through the stages of bringing together ingredients and utensils and calculating cooking times and temperatures? When deciding on purchases we rationalise their usefulness or value with a covert debate. We cannot undertake any novel problem-solving without first labelling our objective with suitable words before we can organise any strategy.

Carl Rogers, with some success as a psychotherapist, treated his clients with minimal intervention. The Rogerian therapeutic dialogue is almost as one-way and 'imaginary' as a child communicating with a Teddy or any other transitional object. The client's struggle, to accurately convey to the listener emotions, unattended past experiences and abstract ideas, *with words,* is the key to therapy. Rogers offered very little input. His occasional verbal responses were mainly *'ums and ahs'*. He gave little feedback at all. His body language was limited to minimal facial expressions – maybe a raised eyebrow or a pursed lip. At key points of discovery he did, of course, share findings with his client.

Why does this type of intervention succeed? It doesn't employ an intermediary process – unlike those apparently found in other talking therapies from deep psychoanalysis to CBT. Practitioners claim these to be essential components in their disciplines. But are they? Are they really necessary? They are not, perhaps, in more informal approaches, but in some other therapies – *definitely not*. The main benefits of all forms of treatment, including art and music therapies, stem from verbalisation. The necessity to find labels for abstractions and to use those descriptions to create structure is the foundation for all types of talking therapy. After conversing with another, labelled anxieties and problems become clearer and shrink. Insights that follow then point to paths for resolution.

I am not decrying any of the more complex forms of analysis. *In extremis*, deep analysis may be the route of choice – the only one, sometimes. And, as far as a professional therapist is concerned, an eclectic approach can be a great advantage. People often present symptoms that dovetail into one particular theory.

When a child speaks to Teddy the dynamic between them is similar to that of adult patients with Carl Rogers. The 'inner voice' of the child appears in Teddy's imaginary responses. And it is when the child is under stress that Teddy mediates as a therapist. The child has to label thoughts and emotions to convey to Teddy. The answers given by Teddy are the child's own choices. Talking them over with Teddy gels those ideas. Teddy's viewpoints help children consider alternative answers formed by their stretched imagination.

My personal childhood experiences, exposed in early chapters here, were substantially shared with my personal therapist, Eduardus Ursus (Big Ted).

I came to realise at an early age how beneficial it was to put my thoughts into words. That was exactly how I learned to cope with my mother's idiosyncrasies – not that I didn't misbehave – far from it. Oddly enough I soon forgot about my isolation in the children's unit – Big Ted was that good a therapist. Those events only reappeared later in life. I realise, now, that secret chats with Big Ted helped avoid conflicts and kept my 'rebellious child' under control. Mainly, though, I shared my joys with Big Ted.

I expressed most of my ideas with him in the early days. He was my transitional object. Later on it was mainly residual attachment. He was always a comfort to have around. As I grew up I rarely spoke to him – just an odd comment from time to time. His loss was unfortunate. It was doubly painful that the precursor to his downfall was that one odd time when I did again relate my day to him. I was definitely angry with my mother but felt guilty when my response was called 'childish'. I may have been mildly clinically depressed for a while after that. I felt isolated and frequently got into sibling fights with my brother and squabbles with my sister.

His loss still colours my behaviour – not aggressively – mainly nostalgically. My wife is frequently in despair with my acquired attachment to transitional objects in the form of old shoes, clothes, etc. It is a genuine barrier to disposal. I feel obliged to keep and mend things – from domestic appliances to cars (I have driven my current one for 20 years to date – its predecessor's mere 15 years was terminated by ferric oxide).

However, Big Ted had taught me how to approach life's difficulties – his bequest to me. Problems are there to be solved not suffered. And isn't it satisfying when they are? People can inherit permanent skills like that, from all forms of talking therapy.

I remain eternally grateful to that young nurse. She replaced my solitude with affection and, crucially, taught and encouraged me how to fill the days with intensive reading. It is a wonderful paradox that illness and isolation offered me such a start in education. The legacy from Eduardus Ursus – to comprehend my childhood issues – still resonates.

The 'secret' component shared by all talking therapies does not in itself explain the universal attraction of Teddy bears and other soft toys.

Much more is at work when a child utilises the trust and affection held for a Teddy and after a period of play enters a phase of interaction with spoken or covert dialogue.

Overt play generates a learning process where the child can find personal space to express ideas and secret thoughts. This is a true oasis in a pre-linguistic desert where a child encounters the frustrations of dealing with the outside world without adequate language skills. When these are acquired the child can overcome the barriers and relate more clearly to others.

As this learning process matures, and with increased verbal acquisition, the child's dialogue with Teddy becomes more structural. Whether internalised or spoken, the *to and fro* conversations equip the child with the tools to resolve anxieties and misunderstandings solely via the child's own thoughts.

Teddy acts as a *psychological mirror*.

Children's ideas are reflected back and forth until satisfied that the conversations – their own ideas – are more harmonious. With greater understanding, balanced conclusions emerge. More concretely, as adults, we learn to resolve difficult choices by drawing up lists of pros and cons. A clear answer usually emerges. If the options are evenly balanced, going on gut-reaction or tossing a coin might be the best solution – reducing angst and with little effect on outcomes.

Many talking therapies rely on labelling abstractions and forgotten emotions and traumas from childhood – with words. When that process is active in childhood (at the source of anxieties) it pre-empts problems in adulthood. Parents can offer encouragement by pretending to communicate and listen to a child's Teddy themselves.

As adults we can be unaware of the effects of some words on our behaviour. Word association can play a useful role in therapy. A single pertinent word can probe the subconscious mind and unearth hidden fears, prejudices and motives.

Advertising agents play on the subconscious in a similar manner and have had to be reined in by legislation – words can be that powerful. An early critique can be found in '*The Hidden Persuaders*' by Vance Packard, an American journalist and social commentator. He proved that, within otherwise neutral presentations, split-second flashes of a word or product covertly registered to promote and motivate naive subjects to purchase those items. Many responded to these prompts, unaware of the subliminal absorption in their subconscious mind. People were induced to buy things – behaving as irrational automatons – on occasion with a herd instinct. That type of advertising was quickly outlawed once exposed.

Words are a potent force in propaganda. Today, politicians speak of 'fake news', 'alternative facts' and 'post truths', etc. Truly evil forces like Nazism took control of entire nations by espousing lies to appeal to the open or covert prejudices of individuals. The childhood mantra of 'sticks and stones can break my bones but names can never hurt me' is completely wrong, wrong, wrong. One only has to focus on the names – rats, vermin, cockroaches – used to define people as a prelude to genocides. Words can humiliate, dehumanise and kill.

Words can be equally used as a force for good. Illiteracy is the enemy of civilisation.

It is normal for a child to talk to a Teddy or an imaginary friend. It is even a sign of sentient intelligence. It should never be discouraged, belittled or stigmatised. Unfortunately that is the case sometimes – and remains so in some quarters when adults engage in talking therapies.

Children benefit from having the freedom to let their imaginations run wild rather than being passively indoctrinated. Some programmes in videos or TV can be both educational and entertaining. But in excess, that manufactured make-believe world can hypnotise a child. It can also run the risk of damage to eyesight and obesity for a child sitting immobile and transfixed for hours on end. Added to that, I find commercial advertisements a disgrace when directed at children and subjecting them to consumerism.

Over the past century we have witnessed the global proliferation of Teddy bears. Today, their influence is stronger than ever. Children readily accept them as mediators. They can also use their bear to test anticipated reactions from parents or others. Bears offer many attributes needed in talking therapists. Non-judgemental, Teddies allow uninhibited ideas to flow. Their touch and unique odour and history with each child, can evoke important memories later in life.

Increasingly over time Teddies and their ilk are viewed as important in child development. Various agencies, police forces and carers, provide them to children at risk from traumatic events. A child will more easily convey abuse, for example, by projecting what they have suffered onto their toy. Professionals have learnt their worth. Instinctively, a wider public will energetically take on a search for a child's lost Teddy.

Leandri Beyers, Warwick D. Phipps & Charl Vorster wrote in Journal of Family Psychotherapy, 2017: *An Introduction to Teddy Bear Therapy: A Systems Family Therapy Approach to Child Psychotherapy.*

These are extracts:

'Teddy bear therapy evolved from psychoanalytic play therapy'…….. 'It entails the telling of a story by the therapist and the child about a teddy bear that is facing difficulties similar to those of the child. Drawing on play and fantasy, the therapist engages the child in a non-threatening way'……..'Together the therapist and the child explore how changes to the teddy and the teddy's relationships in the family, or broader system, ultimately bring about resolution of the teddy's problem. Thus, change is understood at a relational or systemic level.'

Commonplace with children, adults, too, can have strong relationships with Teddies. Many people stay attached to a childhood Teddy that shared all their joys and pains of growing up. Initially, adorably attractive, they can become life-long 'friends' and a reliable source for comfort in distress. It may appear as an affectation but Teddies are owned and cherished by many grown ups in all walks of life. They can be kept as personal keepsakes or heirlooms or in a valuable collection. Some owners use them more openly as perhaps part of their persona. They can serve as a defence mechanism or as an icebreaker against shyness. In particular, Teddies can help physically or mentally challenged people to communicate with others.

In a similar vein, a wide range of Teddy characters appear in the entertainment world and appeal to all ages.
Easily accessible, a Teddy serves as a 'talking therapist' for children. Its influence has grown over the past century. Teddy and Sigmund Freud are entrenched in the public psyche. They have walked side by side since their synchronised beginnings. Teddy's path to its current role parallels the development of conventional talking therapies since Freud's early incursion into psychoanalysis.

When a child turns imaginatively to Teddy in times of stress it acts as a non-judgemental, supportive and friendly 'therapist'. As in other talking therapies, it can help resolve worries with verbalisation and labels. A child may chat to Teddy in thought or orally. With limited vocabulary a toddler may use made up words. No matter – it remains a route to objectively discover solutions.

Is it no wonder – that interacting in all its roles with children *and adults* – the bear has earned such deserved popularity?

CHAPTER FIFTEEN

Now that I'm all grown up, I can buy any old Teddy Bear I want - except the old Teddy Bear I want. William Sternman

Am I being fanciful, seeing a Teddy – an inanimate object – as a truly active psychotherapist?

In the specific arena of pre-linguistic early childhood, Teddy can certainly be seen as a proactive therapist. Consider the three features of labelling, structure and objectivity found in all the various therapies examined in previous chapters. Even before acquiring language a child can identify thoughts with internal symbolism. Conveying that to an inanimate receptor is no problem. But in 'the terrible twos', attempting to do so – without specific words – to parents, siblings and other real people, leads to frustration all round.

Talking things over with Teddy is a stepping-stone to communication and self-identity. It is free from any restriction other than the child's own imagination.

In an ideal world, children should be free to engage in make-believe with Teddies or imaginary friends. It is a testing ground for young children. They can check the validity of ideas and learn to appreciate the effects their own actions have on others. Such simplistic mediators become *psychological mirrors* that reflect the child's responses projected onto them – clearly so with a non-existent twin. Uninhibited chats with Teddy can help a child plan and predict possible outcomes for actions.

When children blame an imaginary friend or Teddy for their own misbehaviour they are in effect testing the reactions of parents or authority figures from a safe distance.

A positive response could be *'Teddy didn't mean it – did he? He upset Mummy and may be sorry.'* That sort of attitude will encourage the child to accept responsibility in future. It removes the fear of punishment – the parent realising the child's ploy is a route to acceptance of wrongdoing. On the other hand a response such as *'Don't blame Teddy – it was you.'* will only alienate and create negative future outcomes. If adults play along with the child the *psychological mirror* is shared and helps create a constructive dialogue free from stress.

In private, talk to Teddy is unrestricted. The sense of invisibility that ensues is a bonus. The benefits of these conversations reach well beyond playtime. Without an audience to consider, other than Teddy, notions can be fully explored. The child learns by trial and error in both thought and action. Self-criticism through Teddy's perceived responses is a form of analysis. Under stress it can act akin to formal child psychotherapy.

When I employed Eduardus Ursus, Big Ted, he was invaluable in helping me sort out my early history and face up to problems at home. His demise was indeed unfortunate. I now realise, of course, that my mother meant well but was misguided by stigma and anxiety. Fortunately Big Ted was around when I really needed him in critical times. I fully appreciate adults revering Teddies who had seen them through tricky times in childhood.

I have noted the affection that many adults retain for their childhood Teddy. Some keep them as companions through the thick and thin of illustrious lives. Had I still had mine he would probably have ended up in a box in the attic until discovered by my children and nosey grandchildren. *If only*. Maybe I would briefly hug him – respond to his smell and texture and the memories we share – and put him safely back in the attic.

I have indicated how talking therapies label abstractions, emotions and subconscious fears. Those labels help create structure for us to dwell on and organise. In pre-linguistic children, communicating with a toy or imaginary friend is a normal stage towards adult thinking. Many children are troubled by subconscious emotions and anxieties. Teddy can be the mediator to help unblock those stresses and promote healthy development.

Have I convinced you – apart from its comfort as a soft cuddly toy – that a Teddy is a genuine psychotherapist? And can be for children and adults alike?

In the great plan of things my childhood experiences were trivial, and are exposed here simply to give a first-hand example of a Teddy acting as a therapist.

Most children, at some time, will have concerns no matter how conducive their environment may be. A Teddy can help to express those thoughts and channel them into constructive action.

Some unfortunate children suffer appalling situations. A Teddy, or his ilk, might be the child's only source of comfort or dialogue and an essential factor in maintaining mental stability. Various agencies such as the police and welfare workers find children can communicate traumas and abuse more freely by projecting them onto a Teddy. The account above of my private childhood trials pales into insignificance against those cases.

Single children without siblings tend to discover other sources for interaction. In the recent past, in China's one child policy, this was undertaken by nuclear families doting on the child. Not always a healthy outcome – childhood egocentricity can become a fixation in later life. Hopefully, many had a Teddy.

Teddy bears are universally loved and cherished. We easily acknowledge their place as a soft toy for children. An outward show of affection for a Teddy projects as a charming or amusing trait in adults – possibly because most of us hold similar feelings more covertly. Perhaps, at last, the more profound influence they have on people's lives can be recognised.

 Before her death in 2017 at the age of 47, Tara Palmer-Tomkinson, the socialite and TV presenter, told the *Daily Mail* about her bear.

'Snowy's been to rehab – he's a bi-polar bear!'
Many years ago, driving down the Avenue Montaigne during Paris Fashion Week, I spotted him in the Dior shop window. 'Turn the limo round,' I shrieked. 'I have to have him. The Eurostar can wait!'

So say hello to Snowy NLMS (Never Leaves My Side) Palmer-Tomkinson, Christian Dior's unique polar bear who's now a fixture in my life. He glories in global glamour – his mode of travel is always first class in my Chanel Jumbo or Hermès Birkin bag.

He's an ice-breaker at airports, popular in cockpits, recognised by pop stars and politicians alike. He drives an F1 Ferrari parked under my piano in London, has his own personalised deckchair in Bali, and has made two visits to rehab (he's a bi-polar bear!).

Snowy is easily jealous and can look furious when he chooses. He brings joy to sick children and is popular with the Starlight and Child Bereavement UK charities, and prepares for public appearances with a blow-dry at Richard Ward, hairdresser to the stars. You probably think I'm crazy to make appointments for a bear at a top London salon.

Well, you're wrong, Snowy makes his own appointments, and what's more, sometimes late at night I hear the strains of Shostakovich coming from my piano. He's an über-talented polar bear. And he's all mine!

That is perhaps a somewhat extreme example.

Teddies can provide comfort and a sense of security to combat loneliness. They can instil confidence, or bring the hope of good luck in superstitious people. Simply cuddling a soft toy has shown to stimulate endorphins. These hormones can help reduce the effects of bereavement, divorce, unemployment and many of life's other disappointments. A welcome shot of endorphins can throw an anchor to reality and challenge morbid thoughts in depression.

As well as lifting moods, endorphins act physically. A similar mechanism is at work. Neuronal responses to corporal damage or inflammation cause pain – pain that can be magnified by other things like fear, loneliness and depression. Perceived pain can be reduced by cuddling a cherished Teddy.

One of the most compelling testimonies to the importance of Teddy bears is evident in the life of Sir Robert Clark. He was a major player in industry. In his extensive career he was a director and chairman of many companies such as British Leyland, Mirror Group Newspapers and *The News of the World*. In the City he was a prominent banker. During World War II he was a paratrooper, captured by the Germans and placed in a prisoner of war (PoW) camp.

He died in 2013. Although briefly mentioned, what was not highlighted in his obituaries is the fact that this 'bearlike, 6ft 4in tall' man was given a Teddy at the age of two and he never left his side throughout his life. Falla, his Teddy, accompanied him to board meetings and during financial negotiations. Sir Robert probably found him an immense comfort and was with him during his internment in the PoW camp.

But the bear was not merely some sort of talisman. Clark's endearment to Falla was proven after the war when he amassed a collection of hundreds of Teddy bears. He demonstrably had a strong attachment to his Teddy and it may only be conjecture – he is no longer with us to ask – but it is highly probable that Falla was his childhood 'therapist' as much as Big Ted was mine.

(Sir Robert's full obituary appears in chapter twenty-five).

CHAPTER SIXTEEN

It is astonishing how many thoroughly mature, well-adjusted grown-ups harbour a teddy bear - which is perhaps why they are thoroughly mature and will-adjusted.
Joseph Lempa

Sir Robert was not alone with Teddy bear obsession.

'A kind-hearted motorist is attempting to get a lost Teddy back to its rightful owner after spotting it abandoned on the A9 dual carriageway', reported The Daily Telegraph in March 2017.

'42-year-old Sally Judd was on her way to drop off her daughter at nursery when she noticed the cuddly toy, and, unable to get the thought of a sad child longing for their bear out of her head, she doubled back on her journey to cross the dual carriageway and rescue it.
Sally, from Blair Atholl, Perthshire, risked life and limb to cross the dual carriageway, which has been dubbed the 'most dangerous road in Scotland' to save the toy.
She parked in a nearby lay-by and waited until there was no traffic before crossing over to reach the central reservation.

What she discovered was a one-armed brown bear with a pink nose and pink feet. She decided to take it home with her and 'pamper' it until it could be reunited with its owner.

She said: 'I spotted it on Tuesday morning on my way to drop off my child at nursery. I couldn't get it out of my head, so I went back to get it. If it were one of my kids who lost it I would want to go back and get it.

'I'm not sure if it lost its arm in the 'accident' but it looks like it is cared for. I thought it had been maybe accidentally thrown out of the window and maybe the parents didn't go back for it.'

To help find the bear's owners, Sally put up an appeal on her Facebook page, where she has so far had hundreds of responses from all over the UK.

On Facebook she shared a photo of the bear recovering from its ordeal with a bottle of 'warm' milk – while another photo showed it looking clean and refreshed, in the hope of letting its owner know that it is being well looked after.

Her post read: 'Please share far and wide. Beautiful Teddy with only one arm found on south bound A9 dual carriageway between Blair Atholl and Pitlochry, Perthshire on Tuesday 28th March 2017.

'Looks well loved so I'm sure there's a little girl or boy out there absolutely in bits over the loss. We've given Teddy some warm milk and she's currently being pampered in the bath. She's keen to get home though, so please share this wherever you are as her owners could be anywhere in the UK because this area is a major tourist area… let's get Teddy reunited with her owner.'

At the time of writing, while more than 1,300 people have shared the post, with over 100 people commenting, the owner is still yet to be found – but Sally's in no rush as she says the bear is more than welcome to stay with her family for as long as it likes.

TEDDY BEAR AND FREUD

This OCD is clearly contagious.

It's a pandemic – from the United States;

'A 10-year-old girl who lost her beloved stuffed bear in the Fort Lauderdale airport shooting will be reunited with him after an anxious plea from her mother.
Rufus, a Teddy bear in a red onesie, went missing among thousands of items during the attack that left five dead and six wounded last week. More than 23,000 items of luggage were left behind during a frantic mass evacuation and a 16-hour airport shutdown.
Airport officials are still working to get the bags back to their owners - meaning Rufus hadn't returned to his Windsor, Ontario home as of Monday night. That's when the little girl's mother, Kim Lariviere, asked for the sheriff's office help on Twitter.
'Looking for Rufus from Terminal 2 D8. Crying daughter cannot sleep. #FLLshooting help!' she wrote. The Broward Sheriff department re-tweeted her message, which has now been shared more than 200 times. But airport officials located the bear Tuesday morning, meaning Rufus will be returned to his owner.

(If you too have been stricken by this OCD and affected by loss, try: -
SITE TO REUNITE; Lost & Found Teddy bear - White Boomerang
https://whiteboomerang.com/lostTeddy)

How about new Teddies? *Bradford Telegraph and Argus* and *The Sunday Times* (23rd April, 2017) carried similar articles on one supplier – here are some extracts:

'They are cute, cuddly, a part of the family and a friend for life.

Teddy bears are a shoulder to cry on when times are tough; they are a companion for tea parties, picnics and for travelling and, more importantly, they are a toy to love and cherish following their arrival. Those passionate about their teddies will be familiar with the pearl of wisdom that says – we don't choose a bear, a bear chooses us. Some say it's in the eyes and it doesn't matter how old you are – Teddy bear owners range from the very young to the more mature. The bears provide companionship for those who can't have pets and even deflated parents suffering from 'empty nest syndrome' have been known to fill their homes with fluffy friends.

Will Morris, co-founded the Charlie Bear Empire with his wife, Charlie. Now based in Cornwall, Charlie and Will's home is the official home of Charlie Bear HQ and the main distribution facility for the whole of Europe and America.

"A lot of my job is going overseas and whenever I go away Charlie always puts one of the little bears into my suitcase and sprays some of her perfume on it," says Will.

"I think there is something nice about knowing you're not travelling on your own." says Charlie. I am 43 - you would have thought I would have grown out of this by now!" Charlie cannot abide the thought of anyone not owning a Teddy bear.

At the time of writing Charlie and Will have been busy at the Bear House Gallery, near Ripon. It displays 2,500 different teddies and 10,000 people from all over the world have visited during its first year. Their Cornwall-based business has a turnover pushing towards £10m a year.

Elaine Moody, a specialist retailer, was in the news when a craze for Paddington Bears developed after the recent films were released. Her toyshop *World of Bears* in Taunton was inundated with orders.

CHAPTER SEVENTEEN

The Teddy Bear is the last toy that we part with. He is all that is left of that lost world where solutions seemed possible and a friend who saw no fault and made no reproach, waited forever in the old armchair. Pam Brown

Who are Teddy aficionados? Surprisingly, many appear amongst the good, the great and the famous.

John Betjeman was inseparable from his bear Archie (full title Archibald Ormsby-Gore). He kept him close from childhood, through University and throughout his life until death. The bear sat next to him on tube trains and buses. He would chastise him in public to the delight of watching children and adults. Apparently he and Archie were the models for Sebastian and Aloysius Bear in Evelyn Waugh's *Brideshead Revisited*.

Delicatessen, one of Peter Bull's bears from his vast collection, played the part of Aloysius in the BBC adaptation on television (1981). The avuncular character actor wrote a book *Bear with Me* (1969) and stimulated a surge in Teddy bear collectors. In a TV interview he promoted the stress reduction and psychological benefits that children and adults alike accrue by owning a Teddy bear.

Elvis Presley just wanted to be 'your Teddy bear', and had a collection of his own.

The Iron Lady, Margaret Thatcher, clearly had a softer side. Apart from her favourite, Humphrey (presumably named after the character in TV's *Yes Minister*), she had a large collection of Teddy bears.

The actor, Richard Briers, was deeply attached to his bear Ragged, beloved by generations of his family.

Dame Barbara Cartland, the romantic novelist, well-known for her extravagant pink outfits, named her bear Prince of Love. He lived in her bedroom and as a result of her amorous attention grew exceedingly worn and tatty. Dame Barbara addressed that by rewarding him with earrings and brooches and other jewellery in gold and diamond.

You may have met some ceramic and metallic Teddy bears created by Grayson Perry in his exhibition at the British Museum in 2011. They were in honour of the artist's companion, cherished since childhood – his now famous bear – Alan Measles. Perry has kept him, these days threadbare, since early childhood. He describes him as his father figure.

Bears can be precious in other ways. When Hedge fund manager Paul Greenwood was charged with a multi-million dollar fraud he was forced to sell assets to cover his legal fees. His collection of Steiff bears sold for nearly $2m, but he could not evade a prison sentence.

When Princess Diana died, hundreds of teddies were left at the gates of Kensington Palace, and eventually found their way to children's orphanages and hospitals.

Prince William bought a 'Harrods' Annual Bear' for his wife Kate soon after she gave birth to Prince George.

Please excuse the continuing name-dropping but these examples have a purpose and a place in later discourse.

TEDDY BEAR AND FREUD

As I mentioned earlier the Daily Mail wrote about celebrities and their teddies, and I quote from some of their other interviews:

Sir Max Hastings, Historian and writer, 67:

'I thought my bear was a boy – but he was a she!'
'On 27th November, 1949, a polar bear in London Zoo named Ivy was delivered of a cub, which became the first of the breed to be successfully reared in Britain. It was named Brumas, an amalgam of the names of its two keepers, Bruce and Sam. The British people fell in love with it, and so did I, then aged four.

My nanny took me to join vast crowds at the Zoo flocking to see the infant bear. We came home with stuffed replicas of Brumas and Ivy, which graced my nursery through the years that followed. Like the rest of Britain, I fondly supposed that Brumas was a boy.

In reality she was a girl – the journalists who attended her first photocall didn't get close enough to establish the infant's sex. Nobody was cruel enough thereafter to put matters right. Brumas died on 17 May 1958, still supposed by all but her nearest and dearest to be a bloke.

My white bears remained my favourite things to take to bed until – well, until I got old enough to realise the possibility of larger female companions. Brumas and Ivy long since went to the great ice floe in the sky, but grandchildren carry on the tradition with a polar bear named Bombo, and a brace of deputy bears called Strawberry and Raspberry, all of whom reside with us.'

I, too, was smitten by Brumas, and made many visits to London Zoo just to see her. Some years after her death I met the Zoo's superintendent, George Cansdale. He told me of his affection for her and how she had been instrumental in bringing him TV fame. She propelled both of them into the Nation's heart.

Jules Knight, Holby City actor, 31:

'I nearly drowned Rory in the pool!'

'I was five and on holiday at the Knoll House Hotel in Studland Bay, Dorset, with my parents when I spotted this sad-looking bear in the hotel shop window. He had tiny little eyes and a floppy golden body, and looked as if he'd nodded off while waiting for someone to love him.

After hours of nagging my parents we visited the shop and he was mine. I called him Rory and took him everywhere – I even had the bright idea of taking him swimming in the hotel pool. Luckily, after drying out on the radiator he lived to fight another day. He slept in my bed at boarding school until I was about 15, when my sisters persuaded me it was time I slept alone. He still sits on top of my wardrobe and he's still in pretty good nick. In fact, he barely looks a day older – unlike his owner.'

Carol Vorderman, TV presenter, 52:

'Bungee and I have our own secret language'

'My mum bought Bungee for me when I was three. We were living in a tiny one-bedroomed flat in Prestatyn in North Wales, and there were four of us, three kids and Mum. We had absolutely no money at all. Mum desperately wanted to buy me something though, and on Christmas Eve she saw this bear in Woolworths. He was discounted to just a few shillings, because he had just the one ear. I fell for him immediately.

Mum then met my stepfather Armido, but when I was nine she ran away from him and we joined my sister Trixie in Leicester where we lived in one room in a horrible bed and breakfast opposite Leicester Prison, with the wind whistling through a smashed window. Apparently I said to Mum one night, "Bungee's sad because he hasn't got a home any more." She said it broke her heart. I even invented a language for Bungee which is used to this day – it's English, but he misses out the last syllable of each word. He's very tatty these days but he reminds me of where I came from, and I just like having him around.'

Janet Street-Porter, Journalist and broadcaster, 66:

'If only all men were like my Mr Ted'

'As a child I hated cuddly toys and dolls, but that didn't stop my parents giving me a nasty pink plastic doll in a party frock for Christmas when I was about eight. We lived in Fulham, west London, and my sister Pat, two years younger, was a softer, sweet child who carefully looked after her collection of dollies.

Nasty Janet quickly ripped the arms off her new friend and pretended there'd been a horrible 'accident' when we were playing doctors and nurses. Mum took the crippled toy to the Doll's Hospital off Fulham Broadway, where she was mended and soon returned with all limbs intact.

From then on, I ignored this alien creature and the only soft toy I would tolerate was a small Teddy that had lost an ear and was bald where it had been dragged around since I was a baby. Battle-hardened Ted managed to cling on to my affections right up to the Christmas when I was nine and unwrapped a giant Meccano set of a complicated crane which Dad and I built in the kitchen, much to Mum's disgust.

I forgot about abandoned Ted until a few years ago when I felt low after my sister died from cancer, and decided I'd like to have a little mascot to keep me company. I spotted Mr Ted sitting on a second-hand toy stall at my local primary school fête in Lofthouse, North Yorkshire. He cost £3 – what a bargain!

It was love at first sight – he's sexless, doesn't answer back and has a non-threatening manner. If only all men were like this! I adore his jaunty pink scarf, tied at a gay angle, which clashes with his red-and-green striped sweater. Mr Ted is my best friend – his quizzical expression is non-judgemental, the epitomy of serenity. He's a role model to aspire to.'

Michael Bond, celebrated as Paddington Bear's creator, 87:

'On Christmas Eve 1956, I bought a bear from Selfridges for my first wife Brenda as a Christmas stocking-filler. We called it Paddington because we lived near that railway station. Not long after, I sat at my typewriter and started writing a story about a real bear discovered at the station, and that became the first Paddington Bear book.

To me, Paddington is very real. It's as if he still exists in the sort of pre-war world that I remember as a child. He's basically a polite bear – when he meets somebody he raises his hat.

Brenda and I divorced in 1981, and since then we've shared custody of the original Paddington. When it's my turn to have him, he sits on my desk, and sometimes my second wife Sue and I take him on holiday. I feel it would be wrong to leave him behind while we're away enjoying ourselves, and Sue feels the same way.

In the early 60s, there was a very nasty moment when I nearly lost him. I'd got off a train when I suddenly realised I'd left him behind. I got straight back on that train and there he was – fortunately no one had picked him up.

I probably wouldn't have created anything like the amount of Paddington books had I never got him back. As it is, there are 13 Paddington storybooks and a lot of picture books – about 80 in total. I hope that after I'm gone he will remain within the family.'

After Michael Bond died, a memorial service was held for him in St Paul's. Appropriately so in more ways than one – the final book Michael had penned, and which was published posthumously, revolved around Paddington's visit to the Cathedral. Hugh Bonneville, who appeared in film versions of the bear's adventures, led the eulogies to the author together with family members. Stephen Fry was among many other well-known arctophiles and a multitude of friends who filled the pews.

I recently trawled through the internet and discovered that many more celebrities are just as enamoured with Teddy bears and can appear quite as eccentric as ordinary people like my elderly relative Rosalind, who when hospitalised had by her side throughout her stay her Teddy, Nicholas (pronounced in an American accent – he only owned a vest).

Gyles Brandreth, 68, writer and broadcaster, was instrumental in establishing the Bear House Museum, at Newby Hall near Ripon with its owner Richard Compton, and presented his collection of over 1,000 Teddy bears to the Museum. They were joined by another 1,500 or more – several world-famous – Teddy bears as a permanent display to the public.

Some bears are famous in their own right.

At Newby Hall you can meet Harry Corbett's Sooty, the original Paddington who starred in the 1970s TV series, Rowan Atkinson/ Mr Bean's knitted Teddy, Fozzy bear from the Muppet Show, the first Pudsey, and others famous in TV.

Politicians' bears reside here, represented by Tony Blair's Lynton and Francois Mitterand's Francois – narcissism or possibly his alter- ego?

Isn't it remarkable that so many people, from the softer 'luvvies' to a hardened financier and war veteran like Clark, have invested so much time and attention to Teddy bears.

Finally, even my mother succumbed. When she stayed with us, after my father died, she came with her cuddly bear. It was not for the children. It remained in her room.

Notoriously fluctuating employment in some professions can induce insecurity. Theatrical people are never unemployed – only 'resting'. Ever vulnerable to comments from critics and peers places them under constant stress – let alone coping with fears of 'drying' or stage fright. At first sight we might think that people of Sir Robert Clark's stature would be immune – but check his career (in Chapter twenty-four) and the personal and commercial risks and responsibilities he undertook. It's no wonder such a diverse range of people may need help to keep face and maintain their equilibrium.

A Teddy can fulfil that role. Why is this so? Why do so many mature and successful people still benefit from anthropomorphism?

CHAPTER EIGHTEEN

Bears are just about the only toy that can lose just about everything and still maintain their dignity and worth. Samantha Armstrong

In the examples I've shown you – not least in my own – Teddies have genuinely acted as psychotherapists. As such, they should no more be ridiculed than trained therapists. Unfortunately both are still stigmatised in many quarters, including those in academic and professional fields. Disdain for psychotherapy can even be found in the medical arena.

But the climate is changing. In the world of psychologists it had done so many years ago. Now mainstream attention is altering attitudes at a pace and addressing, amongst other features, the residual but still damaging stigmatisation associated with mental health.

Today, talking therapies are accepted in most quarters as valuable therapies.

Placing Teddy bears in this field, as I do, will come as a surprise to many lay people. But it has much support within the profession.

In 2010 Claire Harris wrote an article on developmental psychology where she addressed childhood trauma and Teddy bears. I quote some excerpts here:

'This love affair we have with Teddy bears does not stop when we leave our childhood behind us. The Brits, it seems are particularly fond of their bears and in one

Travelodge survey, it was discovered that up to 35% of British adults still take their bears to bed with them. These were primarily women who kept and anthropomorphised their bears from childhood, treated them like friends, sharing problems with them and cuddling them during bad times. Interestingly, up to 25% of British businessmen admitted that they take their Teddy bears with them on business trips.

A lecturer in psychology, Christopher Peterson, asked how many students brought stuffed animals with them to college. He discovered that 'A large number of the 250 students present raised their hands. Thinking I saw a pattern, I asked for shows of hands separately by females and males. Indeed, there was a striking pattern. About 80% of the females had brought a stuffed animal to college, whereas fewer than 10% of the males had done so – or at least admitted to it. But those few guys who raised their hands earned applause from their female classmates. I think they deserved hugs as well, but we don't do that in classrooms at my university.'

There are many psychological reasons for our love of Teddy bears. Not only are they reminders of our innocent carefree childhoods and of the loved ones who purchased the bears for us, but the stroking of the soft fur has also been found to be very therapeutic.

On cuddling Teddy bears, psychologist Corrine Sweet says 'it evokes a sense of peace, security and comfort. It's human nature to crave these feelings from childhood to adult life' (Llorens, 2012). Studies have shown that touching a Teddy bear can lessen the adverse psychological effects of social exclusion and reduce stress (Jarrett, 2011). As a result, Teddy bears are often given to trauma victims, including sexually abused children. Clinical trials have established that considerable comfort is obtained from cuddling, naming and speaking to a Teddy bear. Various police, fire and paramedic departments routinely issue Teddy bears to their officers because they are useful tools in reaching scared, lost, and traumatized children.

Teddy bears come in all sorts of materials but the most popular is mohair plush. This is fur from long-haired goats which is first woven into cloth, then dyed and finally trimmed. Nowadays, bears can be purchased in a wide variety of department stores and over the internet. There are even bear artists who produce unique bears from unconventional materials and dress them in outfits – the market is huge! There are enough bears out there to satisfy even the most avid arctophile.

Steiff is, of course, the most famous producer of bears, ranging from a baby's first bear in soft washable 'plush' to expensive collector items. Even royal families have adored their Steiff bears. In 1908, Grand Duke George Mikhailovich of Russia bought a red Steiff bear for his daughter, Princess Xenia Georgievna, which she called Alfonzo. In 1989 it was sold at Christie's for the then record figure of $19,000.

The world's most expensive bear sold at auction was Steiff's Louis Vuitton bear which fetched an eye watering price of $210,000 and is now housed at the Teddy Bear Museum in Jeju, Korea.

Historical occasions have also been marked by the production of commemorative bears. The most striking was the sinking of the Titanic in 1912 and as a matter of respect for the lives lost, a black Steiff bear was commissioned.

Teddy bears will always be our special friends and who knows, that treasured moth-eaten bear of yours may be worth a small fortune. But after all you two have been through together, would you have the heart to part with it?'

Dr Nathalia Gjersoe, from Bath University wrote the following article on May 9th, 2017 in *Guardian Science*, entitled, 'Why it's (still) okay to sleep with your Teddy':

'What do children really think about their special teddies and what does it reveal about them as adults?

My Teddy is called Mr. T. He is scarred from my childhood voyages — bald patches from sparks in the copper mines of Papua New Guinea, an unravelling nose from being pecked by a giant parrot in Bali, a slight crustiness from having been dropped off a boat in the Spice Islands. On each of those adventures I was only slightly bigger than he was but insisted on bringing him everywhere.

Nobody really knows why some children form strong emotional attachments to a single toy. It is very common in the UK and the USA - 60-70% of children have an attachment object, usually a stuffed toy or blanket. Attachment peaks at around 3-years of age but many children maintain a strong relationship that can last well into adulthood.

We ran a study recently to explore whether children believed their toys had thoughts and feelings. The literature is ambiguous: some studies show that young children are rampantly anthropomorphist, believing that nearly everything has thoughts and feelings. Other studies suggest that children are surprisingly sophisticated and only rarely think of objects as having mental states.

In our study we showed three- and four-year-olds pictures of living animals and stuffed toy animals. We told them stories in which the living animal responded with a feeling and the stuffed toy responded physically. Then we asked them how their own toys with names and faces would react in those situations – more like the stuffed toy or more like the living animal?

Children with no special attachment object and children who had attachment blankets (no faces) believed their toys would respond more like the stuffed toy in the story. Children with attachment teddies, however, believed their special toy would respond like the living animal: with thoughts and feelings.

Children don't divide neatly into those that anthropomorphise all their toys and those that don't. Children only anthropomorphised their attachment object and not other toys they used just as often in imaginary play. Having a very strong emotional bond to a toy seems to make children think about it as more human-like.

There may be long-lasting effects of having such a special bond with a toy in childhood. On measures of unconscious stress, adults are more upset about cutting up photos of their attachment objects than photos of other teddies, their mobile phones or sentimental jewellery given to them by loved ones.

Adults who had attachment objects as children are much more likely than those who didn't to say that collectables (such as moon rocks, original Beatles lyrics and the first light bulb) are 'priceless' or 'invaluable' – that is, beyond any monetary value.

In her delightful book 'Imaginary companions and the children who create them' Marjorie Taylor summarises a wealth of research on children's imaginary worlds. There has traditionally been some concern that imaginary friends are a sign of loneliness, psychological disorders or being out of touch with reality.

However, her analysis of the research shows that children who have imaginary friends are, if anything, less shy, more able to focus attention and have advanced social understanding relative to other children. Children with pretend friends tend to enjoy interacting with others and, when no-one is around to play with, they make someone up.

Attachment objects might serve a similar purpose. One possibility is that children form an emotional attachment to something in the crib with them as they transition from sleeping with their parents to sleeping alone. The object substitutes for some of the emotional security otherwise offered by the mother or father.

There is indirect evidence for this theory. The number of children with attachment objects is higher in societies where children are separated from their parents early (e.g.

UK and the USA) compared to those where children traditionally continue to sleep with the mother into middle-childhood (e.g. Japan).

We recently moved my baby son into his own room and clustered all his toys on the shelves around his crib. The only one he seems to have formed any bond with is Mr. T, my childhood attachment object. After many years in boxes, attics and under beds, Mr. T might finally live again.'

(Dr Nathalia Gjersoe, 2017).

CHAPTER NINETEEN

When everyone else has let you down, there's always Teddy bear. Clara Ortega

Are you convinced? Does my claim that Teddy bears can act as *psychological mirrors* seem fanciful? I hope not. I trust you appreciate the immensely important relationships children have with a Teddy. Why not for an adult?

I have tried to show you how a clear association exists between all forms of talking therapies. One common factor, whatever the mediator, is labelling thoughts and abstract emotions with words. Those key words, whether projected onto Teddy by a child or unearthed during psychotherapy, promote objectivity and lead to resolutions.

Psychoanalytic theories, notably Freudian, cite displacement and projection as defence mechanisms. They are seen as a means of avoiding responsibility for actions or to allay fears. That behaviour can be seen in the earliest of years when children blame Teddies or imaginary friends for their own behaviour. A parent can help in those situations with observations and suggestions directed to the object rather than the child. Without parental intervention the child's words and accusations will eventually bounce back in the *psychological mirror*.

Many adults like Sir Robert Clark kept their childhood Teddy close at hand. In his case it may have been to help express ideas in words before a board meeting or for a number of other reasons – possibly for comfort when a prisoner of war, or as a talisman in battle. That equates to attempts by children to summon up magic.

Some people share feelings to and fro with a Teddy. They possibly acquired that behaviour from a deficit in parental love in childhood, or for any number of reasons. Other people are superstitious and keep Teddy around for luck. Their familiarity can help calm nerves in alien environments – stressful interview rooms or during academic or medical examinations or in hospital wardrooms. Participants in sports or the theatre can have Teddies play a role in routines to help performance. Just another glance through the celebrities listed in previous chapters proves that point.

I could describe the entire adult fascination with Teddy bears as a mild form of eccentricity – even of a pathological nature, ranging from neurotic to psychotic. But that is hardly fair when so many people are engaged. In truth it comes under the umbrella of normality. In some cases it may reside at the very edge but not tumble over into insanity. Self-awareness would dispute that notion.

Teddy characters delight children. Books, films and TV abound with them. Teddy bears have brought smiles to the most serious of faces – Margaret Thatcher and Sir Robert Clark amongst them. People look kindly on people devoted to their aged Teddies. Maintaining those childhood relationships into adulthood may be associated with the stress of vulnerable careers. Many actors point to deep-down personal insecurity attracting them to the world of fantasy. It develops into a refuge as well as a challenge to face their *bêtes noire*. How often have we heard performers state they only feel really alive on stage? In other creative fields we have found John Betjeman, Grayson Perry and Michael Bond, representatives of poets, artists and authors, enamoured with Teddies.

TEDDY BEAR AND FREUD

I have trawled through memories of my own. What gelled my childhood relationship with Big Ted? I must have been attached to him more than I can recall. He was too large to trail about with me but I clearly spent much time with him. His fur-less, threadbare coat was solid evidence of our regular consultations and comforting cuddles.

I was aware when talking to Big Ted it could sometimes be make-believe – sometimes be real. When 'in the zone' with him I suspended my disbelief just as we all do as adults when watching films, TV or in the theatre. The dialogue was private – in a safety bubble – just as it is in formal psychotherapy. We can explore our deepest thoughts in that oasis. The trusted listener, Teddy bear or therapist, not only compels us to label clearly our ideas with words – which we know leads to objectivity and resolution – but encourages us to be open-minded. In that state my deepest thoughts became concentrated – as in a chess match – with no outside interruptions or disturbances.

By the age of seven, before his demise, I realised my chats with Big Ted were mainly one-sided. It was doubly unfortunate that my last words with him were overheard. My mother apart, I blamed myself for being stupid and childish and an accessory to the crime. Would I have suffered his loss less if he simply slowly decayed over a longer period? I was gradually losing interest and growing out of him, when suddenly rushed into the unexpected bereavement. It was, I suppose, just one of those perfect storms we encounter in life.

In therapy we are at liberty to test the likely outcomes of acting upon the wildest of core emotions or prejudices. That precious freedom of expression leads us towards total honesty with ourselves. The input from the therapist can be absolutely minimal. In the case of Teddies it is imaginary. But in both it is critical in maintaining stability when dealing with difficult situations and stresses. Small interventions – slight adjustments, akin to those in a tightrope walker's balancing-pole – can help progress.

As adults our suspension of disbelief degrades with age. We become less involved in story plots – no longer identifying or chiming as much with characters. We tend towards discrimination, criticism or praise in our more mature appreciation of entertainments. Of course that is not a hard and fast rule. Who could enjoy films like *Jungle Book, Paddington Bear or Harvey* (with James Stewart's imaginary large, white rabbit) without a temporary escape from reality?

From the ages of three to seven, without a doubt, Big Ted – Eduardus Ursus – was my psychotherapist and our interactions therapeutic. I quickly lost the residual stressful feelings from isolation and illness. In conversations with Big Ted, I came to terms with difficult episodes. As my reading improved so my vocabulary grew. It became easier to convey nuances, and more accurately describe emotions and past events, drawing on a more expansive lexicon. On revisiting and reviewing old notions with my Teddy I found new insights. Floodlit, these bathed previous problems with clarity – a prime goal in therapy – and put them to bed.

It may seem I have given excessive attention to childhood and Teddies. Surprisingly we are now about to reach full circle with the past century and discover a new Teddy-like therapist.

CHAPTER TWENTY

It's hard to visualize the toys you had fifty years ago - all save bear. He's as clear as if he were sitting on the desk in front of you...of course...he probably is. Pam Brown

Therapists inevitably share some of their patients' worries. Teddy bears – on an imaginary level – can provide unfettered support of this nature. But practitioners operate at a reality level. They absorb some of the stress. It can be a trying day for a therapist when all eight-or-so sessions unearth new problems. Many report getting home after a tough day unable to converse with anyone for an hour or two. The strain of sharing builds up and cannot easily be dispersed. It was not until after I retired – now free of stress – that I became fully aware how true that is.

At times, a therapist's workload or clients' job schedules, family responsibilities, or ongoing costs can become testing hurdles. The shortage of therapists is another well-documented barrier. And unfortunately stigmatisation still turns people away from seeking help.

Is there a future in artificial intelligence (AI) psychotherapy? Current therapy is bound to move in that direction. Simple programmes already exist with fixed regimes to desensitise phobias. Other AI based treatments are in the pipeline. It is in its infancy – used for CBT at present in its limited and structured regimen. In more complex talking therapies it would be revolutionary. Can AI progress to such levels?

Robots could complement the efforts of therapists. A personal one would be more convenient for patients to use. They'd need no appointments and have perhaps more freedom for expression. Chatbots could be Teddy bear-like ears for adults with the added bonus of realistic responses. Alternatively, AI therapy could be conducted via apps in the cloud.

It might seem fanciful that people could respond to a robot. In 2014 a Canadian team created the humanoid, *hitchBOT*, and let it loose on Europe. It fared well, requesting lifts, from many intrigued motorists, to its programmed destinations across Germany and Holland. The experiment was repeated in North America in 2015. But after a few weeks of success the robot arrived in Philadelphia and met a sad end. It was discovered decapitated with all its limbs ripped from its body. Hopefully that will not be the fate of AI therapists.

In the early stages of therapy patients usually carry the baggage of deeply entrenched defences. Initially, dialogues tend to be used to impress or beg for acceptance or to be liked by their therapist. This period is peppered with lies. People lie. It may not be intentional or wilful when part of a defence mechanism. But it is a fact. We all lie on occasion. It can be as white lies to protect or benefit someone. Lies can have other altruistic aims but can also be used to deceive. Deceiving others is not mutually exclusive to deceiving ourselves.

Patience is needed in those early stages of treatment before real inroads can be made. Breaking down a person's defences can be an onerous task and stressful in both camps. It would be wonderful if AI could reduce the strain on therapists in those first dialogues.

It was a massive technological achievement in 1997 when the *Deep Blue* computer beat world champion, Garry Kasparov, in a game of chess. Kasparov later won the next six matches. But chess is a limited challenge. The moves are many – but not infinite – and are clearly structured by rules. The latest count points to over ten million possible games from move one.

It will be far more difficult to create an algorithm to cope with the unlimited variety of tasks involved in psychotherapy. One day, will AI be able to detect nuances in speech? Emotions, facial expressions and body language or 'tells' as in poker? Could they become capable of generating empathy? Could AI detect the subconscious at work? Could it identify free-floating anxiety and locate its motor? Cynthia's mother declared her daughter wicked and addressed her with the nickname Cyn. Could AI register the Freudian significance? Could AI develop the ability to query whether the phonetics of ' Isle of Man' (earlier cited in another case) was geographical or could be transcribed into the 'I love man'?

Algorithms will need robust protocols supervised by trained psychologists and psychiatrists. Could hard-wired technicians ever address the nebulous areas of treatment – the purely scientific mind meld with the 'dark arts' of psychology? I wonder.

Soon, many of those questions will be answered in the affirmative. The benefits will be remarkable. The costs of therapy will reduce with mass production and will be accessible at anytime without any scheduled appointments. Crises will be met as they occur with regular and easy dialogues.

Problems could be 'shared' once enunciated, without the risk of embarrassment or stigmatisation and with less need for defence mechanisms.

Human therapists would act as monitors or mainly be required for fine-tuning, particularly in the later stages of treatment.

Real-life therapy is complicated. Intellectual objectivity and emotional subjectivity can clash. AI therapy will have to be balanced and avoid conflicting with human insights and empathy. Computers are objective not subjective. Psychotherapists are aware of unintended personal influences possible in human dialogues. They can cause setbacks or terminate therapy. Could AI avoid such pitfalls?

CHAPTER TWENTY-ONE

A bear remains a bear - even when most of him has fallen off or worn away. Charlotte Gray

How amusing. The genesis of the Teddy bear in the early 1900s coincided with Sigmund Freud's early work. The resultant development of therapies – from the simple dialogues used by children to the complex psychoanalyses engaged by adults – were synchronised in time. A century on, we could now be arriving at full circle with the merger of an inanimate form and AI that could walk in Freud's and a Teddy's footsteps. The future beckons for this proposed form of psychotherapy. A tangible robot would probably be a more effective source of AI than any online avatar via a computer.

Would AI Teddies' or worry-dolls' responses be an improvement or could they stunt a child's imagination and development? I want to anticipate what this century may bring. It heralds a whole new ball game.

We are at a stage where all sorts of therapies – physical or psychological – cannot cope with demand. An increase in personal longevity is partly to blame but so is the phenomenal increase in our knowledge and abilities. With current technology that increase is exponential as is the clamour for treatments. The demands on the NHS are reaching breaking-point with queues and interminable waits for appointments. The private sector is increasingly expensive. Psychotherapy is stressful enough for both client and practitioner without those obstacles.

AI might answer those pressures. Even as a temporary 'locum' it could relieve the therapist of stress and allow longer and more enjoyable breaks. Therapists could monitor AI from afar, reducing anxieties over leaving clients in crisis. Remote interventions in emergencies would be a safety-net for both parties. Dialogues between AI and client could be recorded for later reflection. In the long term, psychologists would benefit on several fronts. With relaxed holidays and released from some of the donkeywork, therapists would have more time and energy to focus on fine-tuning. Often more rewarding, that area of expertise could lead to greater job satisfaction.

Could clients 'teach' AI? Therapists learn from their patients. Past experience from precedent cases can speed things along. AI could recall such data but could it use it in therapy? Could it note time lapses in speech as pauses in thought, indicating stress? Important features of psychotherapy would be absent. Mutual transference could not exist. The actual presence of another person is a comfort – could AI imitate that?

Therapists gradually develop a rapport with patients. This turns into a form of friendship. A stable interpersonal relationship can help therapists ameliorate lost love, lost ego, rejection, bereavement, loss of employment or loss of status, with empathy and genuine humanity. I have my doubts that AI could ever do that.

Could AI act as 'wallpaper' when appropriate? Therapists can choose to take a back seat to allow clients to organise inner thoughts. A long silence can be extremely noisy. Could AI be capable of such *active* inaction?

Therapists can act as stabilisers. Sometimes people need a temporary anchor to allow them to wallow in their anxieties before they can organise and disperse them. On occasion patients need to take calm re-assessments of their problems – only silently supported by the presence of another person. Could AI function like this and give clarity to ideas without distortion and without direct interference? Could it mimic a sturdy tripod used to prevent shudder in photography?

Could AI learn from clients as in real life therapy?

'Door knob' moments (words or actions from either source at end of sessions) can be revealing. They can give insight or act as a probe. Either way they can promote work between sessions. AI would probably be incapable of highlighting such departing remarks. It wouldn't matter too much in ongoing AI therapy. Enforced intervals between sessions would be absent.

What benefits could AI bring to clients? A personal AI robot would be convenient for people with limited mobility or transport, or who suffer from agoraphobia or during some temporary illness like flu. It could be an easier portal to enter therapy than facing a human practitioner for the first time. Depression, phobias and anxiety could be expressed without fear of ridicule. A likely sense of anonymity could reduce inhibitions and personal censorship. I recall one particular lady who always arrived with an empty shopping bag. I concluded it was to protect herself from stigmatisation and to distract prying eyes from her appointments.

Once accustomed to AI, spontaneity and honesty could be established quicker than with human therapists. It could be a stepping-stone to remove its mystique and instil confidence to approach a real life therapist.

With no fixed appointments and always 'on call' with easy access, AI would address urgent matters immediately. AI would not have an eye on the clock – no 'times up' moments. Those can be damaging and ruin progress made during a session – or be seen as rejection.

Fixed appointments can promote confidence and a sense of security in standard therapies. Regular schedules enhance compliance. However, no such bookings are necessary with AI. People may not commit fully to an AI dialogue. Deficits are bound to arise with AI compared to human interaction.

Compatibility issues with AI programmes would mirror those between human therapist and the client. Some personalities clash – some blend. Would it be easier or harder to relate to a robot? With AI it could be too easy for people to retreat to their comfort zone, when presented with testing proposals, by simply reaching for the off switch. Can the advantages of speed of data retrieval and precise objectivity in AI outweigh the human touch? How would AI deal with role-playing issues?

Would AI be totally accepted at an ethical level? Its algorithms could be embedded with sinister dangers described in *The Hidden Persuaders*. Cyber communication can reduce inhibitions to zero – just consider all the examples of grooming and nudity and sexual content online. Could AI and psychotherapy merge into a close synergy and exhibit empathy – without crossing moral Rubicons? AI must always be programmed not to hurt humans. That could fly in the face of therapy when exposure to psychological pain is inevitable at times.

What can we expect in the near future? Behavioural treatments are much easier to programme than analytical ones. AI could be very effective in the treatment of phobias or other structured behaviour. These simpler forms of therapy are ideally suited to AI. But allowance for underlying causes will need to be built in to AI programmes. It is futile to attempt to cure a phobia only have it replaced by another, generated by the same deeper psychological problems. The spider phobia mentioned in an earlier chapter is such an example.

AI is in its infancy but programmes for CBT are having some success in the USA. The more complex analytical psychotherapy, generated by AI as *Eliza,* is not that successful to date. Many current therapists will dismiss AI with scepticism. Practical barriers will inevitably arise.

AI could also raise employment issues – or more accurately *unemployment* issues. Initial costs will be high but should rapidly reduce with mass production and competition. Ambiguity with phonetics will occur. Such errors could lead to losses in translation similar to those found in foreign product information data or in computerised subtitles on TV and in cinemas.

AI has one great advantage – computers have hard memory banks. Computers 'think' considerably faster than humans. AI could speedily recall past dialogues and link them with current ones.

AI also has its disadvantages. Whilst clients have no need to overcome authority or status imbalance in the initial stages of AI therapy, as is often the case in human transactions, it would be difficult for AI to assess a subject's physical appearance. Any drawn facial features indicating stress, bags under eyes, weight loss, pallid face or painful movement, would be almost impossible to register in even the most sophisticated examples of AI. The subtleties of minor changes in expression or voice would create equally tall orders. Misunderstandings to and fro would occur. Would conflicting body language during conversation be detected by AI or, undetected, result in miscommunication in both directions?

An algorithm can only mimic its appreciation of art or music. It may confirm provenances with forensic analysis, but can hardly respond like humans to subjective stimuli. No matter how deeply we examine a work of art – right down to its smallest particles under an electron microscope – we cannot define precisely why it is considered a masterpiece by such parameters. Similarly AI can never fully respond to human behaviour and emotions.

Computer programmes are invariably fixed and cannot voluntarily adapt to sudden change. Non-programmed situations will arise. Delays in response to *cris de coeur* can be damaging and dangerous. Human contact is very difficult if not impossible to match in AI. Deeper psychotherapies rely on nuances of feeling and empathy. The therapist's personality emerges during treatment as well as the client's. Success depends partly upon compatibility with patients. Innate dissonance leads to failure.

In future, computers could generate competent avatars or holograms of psychotherapists. But could AI ever correlate spoken words with body language? Could it register wriggly feet, when a client is talking, as a sign of lying? Or react to a blush or perspiration or shuffling in answer to a key query? Could AI be programmed to be eclectic and tailor treatments at personal or specific problem levels? We would still retain problems with patient compliance – the 'off' switch being as accessible as the AI.

Operational dangers exist. Some people cannot benefit from AI and could suffer serious damage. Psychoses require an extremely sophisticated approach probably impossible to replicate in AI. It would be risky to help link severe cases to less disordered patients 'in the cloud'. Such interactions can be therapeutic in conventional therapy. They are unlikely to be so in cyberspace. And privacy – what about computer viruses or hackers? Personal data could be vulnerable. AI dialogues could be used for commercial or political espionage, if not encrypted. Access to AI has to be limited to the client and the monitoring human therapist with secure passwords, etc.

As an adjunct to therapy, AI could be a useful tool to accurately score questionnaires, help detect pathology, and offer objective analyses. I can foresee AI developing newer forms of therapy when successes from errors or unforeseen novel approaches occur by chance.

CHAPTER TWENTY-TWO

A bear grows more alive with age. No one with one ounce of sensitivity could ever consign a bear to the dustbin. Johnnie Hague

We have come full circle with Big Ted – but where from here? Child and Teddy is a simple relationship. Children have few defence mechanisms, are more honest with clear but limited ideation and verbal reasoning. A Teddy modified with AI might have limited advantages over a standard one. Young children 'converse' in an imaginary way. Their overt language is limited and often idiosyncratic – and interpretations can vary. Communication with toys can be in thought alone or via symbols. AI in a Teddy bear might negate its role in child development.

An important consideration for adults, when choosing a real life therapist is compatibility. What choices will there be in AI? Can we overcome the many inherent problems we are currently aware of and the multitudes that will arise as we attempt AI's development? If we can, its robotic presence will have all the attributes of that childhood Teddy. Some of the more sophisticated needs in our more mature years could be met with AI.

Those two forms of talking therapies have parallel mechanisms. The child's own imagination mediates and tests new ideas in a safe environment with Teddy. That facility is more pronounced in our early years than when adult.

Innocence and a lack of embarrassment over errors are stronger in children than in grown-ups. We become more rigid as we reach adulthood. Old dogs – new tricks, we find it more difficult to acquire new languages and have less free imaginations. AI could be the mediator to remedy adult reluctance to talk openly about issues without awkwardness and create a similar platform for adult privacy as a child has with a Teddy.

We have delved through the development of a wide range therapies initiated in the early 1900s. After a full century Freud and Teddy bears have influenced psychotherapy in parallel. The two paths that began almost simultaneously have taken similar directions and are beginning to merge into one. The child-Teddy bear dialogue with a toy – imaginary, with limits imposed by illiteracy and inexperience in childhood – compares to adults talking to a responding avatar, robot or other AI, whether in a physical form or in the cloud.

One single thread that has run through every talking therapy will persist in the future – however AI develops. Patients will verbalise inner thoughts, identify, label with words and objectively address problems through AI dialogues. That same feature has been the core of all talking therapies over the past one hundred years. Unless built into AI programmes it cannot succeed as a therapy. Forced to explain, in words, to a trusted listener what is going on in the mind is the key to success in every form of talking therapy.

We have arrived at the end of our stroll through a century of talking therapies. In recent years the pace has quickened. We are now beginning to accelerate into a sprint but with no finishing line. Can AI pick up the baton?

The realistic probability of robots aiding, or even overtaking, today's therapists will inevitably come to fruition at a fast pace. Human knowledge and technical skills are increasing at an exponential speed. Another hundred years from now the world will be a very different place. AI will certainly evolve and create therapies we cannot currently envisage. Nevertheless, a Teddy bear and Freud are likely to remain influential and continue their journey together through the present century.

CHAPTER TWENTY- THREE

As a speech therapist, I scored over anyone in getting withdrawn children to talk to me – I would fix Ted straight in the eye and carried on normal conversation. Helen Thomson

Whatever the future brings for talking therapy – whatever form it takes – its end-game will follow the same route. After unearthing traumas, abstractions and emotions, and conveying them newly labelled to a sympathetic ear, fresh insights will emerge and inevitably create more accurate narratives for past misunderstandings or to clarify current situations. That core process will always feature in the final stages of treatment regardless of the initial choice of talking therapy. Whether engaged with a professional, a cyborg, an avatar, a chatbot or a Teddy, talking therapy has to take the same final path to achieve success.

The wide diversity of treatments is irrelevant. The *psychological mirror,* when a child simply chats to a Teddy, leads to self-reflection. In deep analyses, hidden subconscious material is brought to the surface by trained professionals for profounder discussion. Throughout the entire spectrum of disciplines we have looked at, new labels and strong objectivity create structures that bring therapy to its conclusion.

Since the earliest days of the past century talking therapies have evolved and become more sophisticated. During the same period a toy, inspired by an American President's empathy for bears, has developed into many cherished forms. A Teddy bear has become a natural talking therapist for children and in some instances for adults, too.

Teddy bear and Freud might, at first sight, have seemed an odd couple. I see them integrated as precursors to the entire spectrum of current and future forms of taking therapy. I hope you agree.

CHAPTER TWENTY- FOUR

Anyone who has looked a teddy bear in the face will recognize the friendly twinkle in his knowing look. Harold Nadolny

If ever there was proof of the benefits of psychotherapy – partly forfeiting my privacy and exposing it directly to you – this is it!

Without question all talking therapies share the one common factor of verbalising inner thoughts and emotions. In fact, across all the variety of treatments available it may be the sole component behind successful therapy. The Freudian approach is intellectually stimulating but is it any improvement on simply chatting to a neutral friend, a good listener, a non-interventional therapist like Carl Rogers (or even Teddy), or in the foreseeable future a programmed avatar?

Are mediating structures really necessary to achieve fresh objectivity, new insights and clearer cognition? All talking therapies address destructive thoughts. They help locate nebulous elements attached to childhood mishaps, trauma or social or financial distress. Descriptions of abstract associations and emotions, to the listener, generate clarity to the speaker. Whether employing a complicated or a simple approach the one goal is to identify and resolve the problem with verbal reasoning.

As a generalisation I believe that verbal interaction with others – finding words to describe feelings and abstractions – is the key to open any talking therapy door. In childhood a Teddy is the ideal therapist. He is not judgmental, is not didactic, he listens attentively without interruption and allows a free flow of ideas, and is supportive. Good therapists, whatever their particular discipline require those qualities.

'How do you feel?' 'Can you try and put it into words?' 'Describe exactly what happened.' Those are questions frequently asked. In many cases, however, the deeper probes found in the more sophisticated therapies are necessary – sometimes transiently – sometimes long term. Freudian analysis still has its place.

The outcome of talking therapy of any description is often a lesson for life. Future crises or even mundane or financial problems can be tackled with the acquired skills learned when resolving past difficulties. The verbal structures that led to better cognition and objectivity can become a permanent scaffold of support imbuing confidence to meet worries head-on and with open discussion with others.

At its simplest level, talking to other people can identify and correct long held errors and ideas.

The time, when my total egocentricity gave way to the recognition of the needs of others and their existence – came into clear focus. I recalled when I realised that everything I did affected other people.

I located other critical points in my childhood. One day, meat was food for thought, rather than digestion. It became an early moral dilemma – breeding then slaughtering animals. Beef was no longer a neutral word. It conjured up the picture of cattle innocently grazing in green pastures – and we kill them for food!

I have made several personal insights as adjuncts to this narrative. My long held residual issue with my mother has completely vanished. The suppressed pain over Big Ted has been excavated and has disappeared. I finally resolved any remaining subconscious resentment and came to terms with his loss whilst writing this book. I have finally accepted 'a locum for him', having been reminded by my eldest daughter (the one who lost the blue rag) of my mother's attention to her replacement Teddy, named Podgy.

Podgy arrived in my daughter's infancy and accompanied her through school, university, marriage and motherhood. I knew that but was unaware – or had forgotten – that my mother had made a waistcoat for Podgy during my daughter's teens. And 'Grandma talked to Podgy', I was told recently. I had had no idea.

For my recent birthday my wife was persuaded, with a little prompting from my daughters, to buy a large Teddy that I had frivolously suggested to them might finally replace Big Ted. I am not in a second childhood – I accepted him as the resident Grandpa Teddy for my grandchildren. They love him and say 'good morning' and 'good night' with cuddles and delight, and with sadness on saying 'goodbye'. I am no longer a closet arctophile, but perhaps project it onto the grandchildren. It remains partially hidden. Yesterday, as I sat and glanced across my lounge, it was comforting to see Grandpa Teddy in his armchair.

Did he *really* smile at me?

CHAPTER TWENTY-FIVE

A bear remains a bear - even when most of him has fallen off or worn away.
Charlotte Gray

E arlier on, I promised you two specific biographies in greater detail. I hadn't forgotten – here they are.

My dear friend, Dr Barry Berkovitz – a world authority on head, neck and dental anatomy, and honorary curator at the Royal College of Surgeons of England – has a soft spot for bears. When he discovered I was writing something on Teddies, he offered me the following excerpt from an article he had written. It gives an account of Winnie's life and her association with the College.

'Lieutenant, later, Major Harry Colebourn was born 1887 in England. He travelled to Canada in 1905, as an 18-year-old and qualified there as a veterinary surgeon in 1911. He gained an appointment with the Department of Agriculture, Health of Animals Branch, in Winnipeg. He also joined the 18th Mounted Rifles and was seconded to the Cavalry the following year.

Already a trained officer when World War One broke out in 1914 he was given leave of absence from the Department of Agriculture.

He left Winnipeg by train on 23rd August, bound for Quebec to join the Canadian Army Veterinary Corps. On 24th August the train stopped at White River, Ontario, where Harry purchased a small, dark brown, female bear cub for $20 from a trapper who had killed her mother. He named the cub, Winnie, after Winnipeg, his home town. In October 1914 he and Winnie sailed to England.

Winnie remained with him at the Second Canadian Infantry Brigade Headquarters and became a Mascot to the Canadian Army Veterinary Corps. She became a pet to many of the soldiers and would follow them around like a domestic dog in their off-duty hours – on Salisbury Plain.

There are numerous photos taken of her with the men, some of these pictures becoming a keepsake for them to treasure. She would sleep under Harry's cot in the tent on Salisbury Plain although, as she got bigger, Winnie loved to climb the central pole in the solders' tent and give it a shake. There was concern the tent might collapse and she was subsequently tethered outside!

The photo, next page, of Winnie playing with Harry comes courtesy of Wikipaedia.

Winnie with Harry Colebourn

When the war ended Winnie moved to London Zoo. An early visitor was Christopher Robin Milne (1920-1996) who came with his father, A.A. Milne. Christopher added 'Pooh' to Winnie's name and renamed his beloved Teddy bear Winnie-the-Pooh. The name Pooh came from his pet swan. Apparently Christopher Robin had a birthday party at the Zoo with some of his friends. It was held in Winnie's den. The little bear liked condensed milk, which led to his obesity. No record exists of the bear having a taste for honey, a particular favourite of Pooh's in Milne's books.

Through his father's books, Christopher Robin, became one of the most famous children in the world. He was always associated with the little boy with the golden hair who 'is saying his prayers'. This proved to be almost a curse during his lifetime and he rebelled against it. Sadly, because of this seeming exploitation, he subsequently broke off all contact with his father. Like his father, he attended Trinity College, Cambridge and in 1974 wrote a widely read autobiography entitled The Enchanted Places. He became the owner of a successful bookshop in Dartmouth.'

(Chris, my Devonian son-in-law, met his namesake and treasures the copy of 'Pooh' signed to him and his childhood Teddy).

'Harry Colebourn returned from the war and visited Winnie at the Zoo whenever he was on leave. Realising how popular she was with children and adults, Harry decided not to take her back to Canada as he had planned, but on December 1st 1918 donated her officially to the Zoo.

Winnie lived a long and full life there. Although she had cataracts in both eyes and did not want to take her pills for osteoarthritis, she was otherwise content. On May 12th 1934 she died, when she was 20 years old, a good age for a bear. Harry Colebourn was kept informed of her progress, including her death. She predeceased him by 13 years. She was so loved by all that she had an obituary in the London press.

When Winnie died the London Zoological Society donated her skull to the Odontological Collection at the Royal College of Surgeons of England. Unexpectedly, it added another case for the study into the diseases of teeth in animals (her love of condensed milk to blame). Winnie's skull was held in the Museum's stores alongside other bear skulls until it was recently highlighted in a Collections Review as a specimen that would be of much interest to the public. It has since been put on display in the Hunterian Museum.'

Unfortunately the Hunterian Museum was recently demolished in a redevelopment scheme. Winnie's skull awaits a new future.

The second biography is Sir Robert Clark's full obituary that appeared in *The Daily Telegraph*:

'Sir Robert Clark died 3rd January 2013 aged 88.
An habitué of numerous boardrooms, Clark stepped in to chair British Leyland when Sir Ronald Edwards died and — more controversially — Mirror Group Newspapers after the demise of Robert Maxwell.
The bearlike, 6ft 4in tall Clark combined good manners and a readiness to listen with a mastery of his subject and an ability to dismiss wild ideas without humiliating the proposer. But he was not a man to cross, and in the bruising world of takeovers he was fearless: Clark was one of the few men brave enough to sue Rupert Murdoch for libel, when Maxwell was fighting Murdoch in 1969 for the control of The News of the World.'
'*Despite being beaten to the paper by Murdoch, Maxwell retained Clark as banker to his British Printing Corporation and they became friends. Clark became a director of MGN in May 1991 after the company's £201 million flotation. He tried to make*

Maxwell follow orthodox business practise, and "until quite close to the end, he never did anything I asked him not to do".

Clark said later that, although there had been 29 "unusual" payments totalling £230 million to private Maxwell companies over a year, no director had the evidence to challenge their honesty. DTI inspectors eventually determined that Clark and Alan Clements, the former ICI director who became his deputy, should, as the two non-executives, have acted on these warning signs.'

'After Maxwell had gone missing from his yacht the Lady Ghislaine off the Canary Islands that November and his body retrieved from the sea, a month elapsed before his companies were found to be in trouble. Clark stayed as attempts began to sort out the mess; then, in June 1992, he was asked by administrators of the Maxwell companies to take the chair. By then MGN had written off £492 million as the price of Maxwell's fraud on the company and its pension fund, declaring a £388 million loss for the year. MGN sought relisting of its shares and Clark set out to rebuild its board. In October 1992 the former Today editor David Montgomery was appointed chief executive, and the pro-Labour media tycoon Lord Hollick a director.

Hollick lasted just five months before unwisely taking on the chairman. Clark observed: "He mistook politeness for weakness. It is always a big mistake." He stayed in the chair at MGN until 1998.'

'Robert Anthony Clark was born on January 6, 1924 in London, the younger son of a sales engineer. At Highgate, he was head boy and captain of football and cricket during the wartime evacuation to Westward Ho!

Robert went up in 1941 to King's College, Cambridge, to read Modern Languages, but left after a year — during which he won a soccer Blue — to join the Royal Navy. Given a desk job because of his colour-blindness, he joined the SOE.' (Special operations executive).

Surely, you ask, I could have come up with a more suitable example? Where is the Teddy?

TEDDY BEAR AND FREUD

Perhaps Dame Jenni Murray? The broadcaster and writer was chosen for comment on Teddy bears by the *Daily Mail*. This is her story:

'I couldn't eat or sleep for weeks when I lost Teddy.'

Jenni Murray lives with her Teddy bear at her home in the Peak District.

Teddy was a present from my grandparents, who brought him to the hospital where I was born, and since then he's sat in my cot, then on my bed and now he has his own seat in my bedroom. My mother named him – rather unimaginatively – Teddy.

The worst incident of my childhood was when he was lost. I took him to the shops and must have popped him down for a minute and forgotten him, only remembering when I got home and started wailing in panic. We went everywhere to try and find him. No one could help. He was gone for two weeks.

I couldn't eat or sleep and Mum suggested a replacement. I would have none of it. Then a policeman came to the door. Someone had found him in the shop and taken him to the police station. The police had heard in the village about this heartbroken little girl and tracked us down. I can still remember the absolute joy I felt when my mother put him in my arms. He's 63 years old now. He has companions with much more impressive pedigrees who've been given to me over the years by people who know my fondness for the breed. But he's the one I still see every night, smiling at me with his kindly eyes. Still my most treasured possession.'

That's more like it you may say, but please, continue with Sir Robert.

'After rigorous training in Scotland, he was parachuted into northern Italy early in 1943 to train partisans and carry out sabotage — with his lifetime companion, his Teddy bear Falla, tucked into his battledress.

This was the sole mention of a Teddy in his obituaries.

Dropped 50 miles from his target, he landed in a tree.

Clark took to his task with gusto. "Blowing up railway engines", he recalled, "was very great fun." He went on to conduct beach reconnaissance from a canoe, reporting to Baker Street via an onshore SOE wireless operator, Marjorie Lewis.

Clark's war ended when he and four partisans were discovered in a haystack by a German patrol. He became "an expert on the state jails of northern Italy" before being moved to a PoW camp in Germany.

Marjorie had no idea if he was alive until, months later, a message came in plain English (in total breach of the rules): "Bob sends love to Marjorie." Freed as the war ended, Clark wired her: "Arriving London from Germany. Meet me." They met, shook hands — and later married.'

'Demobilised in 1946 with a DSC, Clark planned to go to the Sudan until his former CO, Hilary Scott, invited him to join his law firm, Slaughter & May. Working exclusively for merchant banks, he became a partner at 29. He was blooded in the Hadfields-Millspaugh saga, one of the most bitter of takeover battles.

In 1961 Clark joined the fast expanding merchant bank of Philip Hill, Higginson, Erlanders, and was soon offered a directorship. Then a merger with M Samuel & Co created Hill Samuel, one of the City's two largest merchant banks, embracing shipping, insurance and investment worldwide.

As head of its issues and mergers department, Clark was involved with GEC's bid for AEI and its merger with English Electric, and worked on a series of takeovers with Ernest Harrison of Racal. When in 1967 the Astor family sold The Times to Lord Thomson, Clark tossed Thomson for the final £50,000 of the price on Lord Astor's behalf. Thomson lost, and Clark kept the half-crown mounted on a silver stand.

In 1969 Clark accepted his first assignment for government: a seven-year stint chairing the National Film Finance Corporation. He later served on the committee representing Rolls-Royce's creditors as the company was nationalised.'

'From 1973 to 1980 he chaired the Industrial Development Advisory Board. After Tony Benn overruled its objections to his Industry Department funding the workers' co-operatives at Triumph and Fisher-Bendix, Clark said the Board would "soldier on" in hope of restraining him. Benn bore him no animosity, appointing him in 1974 to Sir Don Ryder's committee on the future of British Leyland. In 1976 Clark took the chair of the company as a stopgap, but stayed for more than a year — during which time BL, beset by strikes, effectively went bust and was nationalised — before handing over to Sir Michael Edwardes.

He stayed on BL's board, and in 1986 shuttled to and from Detroit in an attempt to get General Motors to improve its offer for Leyland Vehicles. The deal was killed by a public outcry over the proposed inclusion of Land Rover.'

Please stick the course. You will see why this long testimony intrigued me.

'In 1976 Clark had succeeded Sir Kenneth Keith as Hill Samuel's chief executive, setting its sights on expansion overseas; from 1980 he was chairman. He rebuffed a takeover approach from Merrill Lynch, but with the onset of "Big Bang" in 1986, when UK financial markets were deregulated, he concluded that Hill Samuel was too small to go it alone.
Faced in 1987 with a hostile approach from Kerry Packer and Australia's FAI Insurances, Clark agreed to a takeover by the Swiss bank UBS. Weeks later, UBS pulled out and that October TSB acquired Hill Samuel after the sale of its corporate finance department to Barclays collapsed. Clark was deputy chairman of TSB until 1991.
Other companies he chaired included Beecham, Imperial Metal Industries, Marley (its first non-family chairman) and United Drapery Stores, where he fought off a bid from Heron before accepting one from Hanson. Among his directorships were Bowater,

Eagle Star, Marchwiel (later Alfred McAlpine), Racal Telecom (later Vodafone) and Shell. From 1976 to 1985 he was a director of the Bank of England.

In 1993 Clark founded his own investment bank, Rauscher Pierce & Clark (now RP&C International), putting up 20 per cent of the equity. Two years later he took the chair of the insurance brokers Lownes Lambert (later Lambert Fenchurch), once part of Hill Samuel, on the sudden death of Richard Shaw.'

No further mention of Teddies. But what a career.

'*Clark's home for almost 50 years was a house in Surrey designed by Lutyens for Gertrude Jekyll ("the best investment I ever made"). He was a keen collector of antiquarian books, and retraced the route of one of Cook's voyages.*

He was one of 29 former SOE members who in 2010 held a reunion at the Imperial War Museum, followed by a dinner with the Princess Royal at the Special Forces Club. Clark was at various times chairman of the Review Body on Doctors' and Dentists' Remuneration; vice-chairman of the Salisbury Cathedral Spire Appeal; and a director of the English National Opera. He was knighted in 1976.

Robert Clark married Marjorie Lewis in 1949; they had two sons and a daughter.'

His obituary has the flimsiest of connection to a Teddy bear. But I specifically focussed on Sir Robert Clark.

It probably came as no surprise to you that someone as empathic as Jenni Murray is attached to her Teddy bear. But Sir Robert Clark? After reading his long obituary, who would have believed that a man with such a spectacularly successful and weighty career would intimately associate with a child's toy? And as I mentioned earlier, he was so enamoured that he amassed a large collection of Teddy bears later in life.

The DailyTelegraph cited the stellar achievements of the man in great detail. He was clearly a hardnosed negotiator in business and a brave soldier in the war. He encountered massive challenges in the financial world and apparently accepted his responsibilities with ease – a highly respected man, indeed.

Falla, his toy bear, was only mentioned once, a fact that could be easily missed, or if noted, considered a trivial oddity. However, to me, his attachment to his bear was pure gold. It was further proof, if ever needed, of how important Teddies can be to even the most serious of people.

APPENDIX

Earlier, I did suggest that you could, if you wish, just scan the text covering the range of various therapies. But if you did I wouldn't like you to take my word for their connection with each other and with Teddy bears. Even if you are fully familiar with most therapies I would still like you to feel and absorb that relationship.

Now that I have made those claims you might wish to challenge them. If you do, please, at the very least, spend some time over the simplified tables I've made to underscore them. They could dispel any misunderstandings between us. I hope they will help clarify the connection of orthodox therapies with Teddy bear dialogues.

The core features in each discipline are presented for easy comparisons. When you do so, please keep an eye on the first table for a child engaging in conversation with a Teddy bear and compare it to all the other tables.

The proof of the commonality within all forms of talking therapy *including talking to a Teddy bear* emerges without compromise in these tables.

Please take note of the final trio of boxes (7), (8) and (9). You will find similar conclusions in the other examples that follow.

CHILD and TEDDY BEAR

(1) CLIENT (Child) Traumas, stress, sub-conscious or otherwise, create a need to uninhibitedly talk things over with someone.	(2) MEDIATION Relating inner thoughts to Teddy.	(3) EXAMINATION Checking Teddy's responses (imaginary reflections in the *psychological mirror*).
(4) THEORETICAL DYNAMICS A conversation develops to and fro with the imaginary responses.	(5) ANALYSIS Mulling over Teddy's replies (i.e. the child's own range of interpretations).	(6) VERBALISATION Talking to Teddy out loud or in thought.
(7) LABELLING Accurate words – or the child's idiosyncratically, invented words or symbols – used in conversation, label inner thoughts, abstract feelings, and ideas.	(8) OBJECTIVITY Labelled by words, etc., overt behaviour and abstract ideas can be clearly identified. This leads to a new, more accurate assessment of situations.	(9) STRUCTURE A bridge between overt and inner thoughts creates promotes a clearer picture of events. This helps to develop coping ploys. These become learned behaviour for future crises.

Freud's ego, super–ego and id dynamics form the main focus of enquiry into what we know as Freudian Psychoanalysis. Full blown, it is a complex and time-consuming process – full of nuances and subtleties – and undertakes difficult excavations of the subconscious mind. Such explorations may be essential in severe and complicated cases of mental illness. For inquisitive people, fortunate enough to have the time and money, deep analysis can lead to greater self-awareness, insightfulness and confidence with resultant life-long benefits.

Therapists assign the source of the analysand's problems into Freud's triadic format. As the analysis progresses, thoughts and actions are identified as an ongoing subconscious conflict between the self (ego) and the instinctive drives of the id. This battle is further moderated by the super-ego – more or less, the conscience – built over time by learning experiences, punishment, authority figures and role models, parenting and such. The aim of therapy here is to shed light onto behaviour by bringing these components into balance. This mediation re-labels the client's accounts of events, investigates slips of the tongue or dreams, and forms new structures to promote more objective thinking. These altered theoretical dynamics help establish new patterns in real life behaviour.

Psychoanalysis unearths possible subconscious roots behind thoughts as the client and therapist exchange ideas in protracted conversations over long periods of time. During this process of verbalisation the client labels thoughts, abstract feelings and actions to create newer, more accurate, versions of experiences.

Many modernists dismiss his approach as pure fantasy and some even suggest quasi-religious components at work. Strangely enough we now have evidence that his proposition is more scientific than originally thought. On investigating the action of the brain's limbic system we see empirical support for Freudian theory with drive centres that mimic the id, and a hippocampus that functions very much like the theoretical super-ego. Enough of that argument – it is redundant here.

FREUDIAN ANALYSIS

(1) CLIENT Presents with problems.	(2) MEDIATION Client's account is recorded and analysed with the familiar triad of the Ego, Super-ego and Id of the subconscious.	(3) EXAMINATION Behaviour, including dreams, slips of the tongue, is assigned mainly to those subconscious elements.
(4) THEORETICAL DYNAMICS A pattern of behaviour is established for further examination.	(5) ANALYSIS Therapist expounds the possible subconscious roots behind actions.	(6) VERBALISATION Client and therapist exchange ideas in long conversations.
(7) LABELLING With new words, client is able to label abstract thoughts, feelings and actions. Subconscious ideation is brought into the light.	(8) OBJECTIVITY When labelled, overt behaviour and its connection with abstract ideas can be clearly identified.	(9) STRUCTURE A new, more accurate, assessment helps client resolve problems.

Jung suggested the repressed ancestral past is a proponent controlling behaviour, personality, and thoughts. Here the ego and personal unconscious and the collective, ancestral or existential unconsciousness, interact to create a platform to assign unresolved feelings and thoughts to objective structure. Jung viewed people's problems as originating from divisions between the ego's demands and personal and ancestral unconscious experiences. He saw symbolism and transcendental elements behind overt thinking and behaviour.

Jung claimed that inherited or acquired features dominate behaviour and are partially responsible for inappropriate thoughts.
Symbolism here is analogous to words in the 'labelling' stage prior to analysis. Repetitive symbols indicate connections. Jung's ideas of synchronicity revolve around universal symbolism.

JUNGIAN ANALYSIS

(1) CLIENT	(2) MEDIATION	(3) EXAMINATION
Presents with problems.	Symbolism and transcendental elements create divisions between the ego and personal unconscious and the ancestral unconscious.	Identification of inappropriate thoughts driven by partially inherited or acquired features. These are claimed to dominate people's behaviour.
(4) THEORETICAL DYNAMICS A pattern of behaviour is established for further examination.	(5) ANALYSIS Therapist expounds the possible subconscious roots behind actions.	(6) VERBALISATION Client and therapist exchange ideas in long conversations.
(7) LABELLING Client is able to label thoughts, feelings and actions with new words.	(8) OBJECTIVITY When labelled, overt behaviour and abstract ideas can be clearly identified.	(9) STRUCTURE A new, more accurate, assessment helps client resolve problems.

Adler had a different explanation for overt behaviour. Images of an ideal self and the real self, fighting this inferiority complex, brought the psyche into conflict. Practitioners here search for such subconscious roots with intense examination during long dialogues and many sessions with clients. If these ideas are accepted this novel structure can name feelings that, previously unidentified, generate angst in patients. This can facilitate working through problems and give insight to current and future stresses. The Adlerian sense of holistic personality has been said to lead on to later CBT.

ADLERIAN ANALYSIS

(1) CLIENT Presents with problems.	(2) MEDIATION Adler's theory suggests an inferiority complex battles with an image of the ideal self and the real self.	(3) EXAMINATION Subconscious thoughts and overt behaviour are explained by that conflict.
(4) THEORETICAL DYNAMICS A pattern of behaviour is established for further examination.	(5) ANALYSIS The therapist expounds the possible subconscious roots behind actions.	(6) VERBALISATION Client and therapist exchange ideas in long conversations.
(7) LABELLING Client is able to label thoughts, feelings and actions with new words.	(8) OBJECTIVITY When labelled, overt behaviour and abstract ideas can be clearly identified.	(9) STRUCTURE A new, more accurate, assessment helps client resolve problems.

Gestalt therapy is based on the idea that 'the whole adds up to more than the sum of the parts'. Gestalt therapists use the ideas offered in this discipline to help clients take a holistic view of their problems. This subjective process leads to a more directional approach to issues. It can take into account many facets of behaviour within the personality as well as relationships past and present. Delving into clients' actions and thoughts, they sought to name these elements and weave them into a larger tapestry to represent a more comprehensible account of behaviour.

GESTALT THERAPY

(1) CLIENT Presents with problems.	(2) MEDIATION A combination of tiny factors can be behind chaos and unhappiness.	(3) EXAMINATION Delving into overt behaviour can reveal that interaction.
(4) THEORETICAL DYNAMICS The focus is on seemingly minor behaviour patterns.	(5) ANALYSIS How do these create a larger tapestry?	(6) VERBALISATION Client and therapist discuss the interactions.
(7) LABELLING Client is able to label thoughts, feelings and actions with new words.	(8) OBJECTIVITY When labelled, overt behaviour and abstract ideas can be clearly identified.	(9) STRUCTURE A new, more accurate, assessment helps client resolve problems.

In transactional analysis (TA) the therapist helps the client become aware of role-play to examine how his personal parent, child and adult viewpoints vary and interact with each other in diverse situations. Generally the client's inappropriate role-playing is addressed. Progress can also be made when the therapist mimics and addresses those roles to expose weaknesses in people's relationships. Misunderstandings, or poor – even hostile – attitudes from within the subject's circle, can appear.

Once established, the dialogue in TA acts as a bridge to reality. The focus is on learned behaviour rather than the subconscious. Experiences from the past can trigger memories when seemingly similar situations arise. This can elicit inappropriate responses in the present. The patient becomes aware of this mechanism and learns to identify and modify reactions towards a more serene approach to life.

TRANSACTIONAL ANALYSIS

(1) CLIENT	(2) MEDIATION	(3) EXAMINATION
Presents with problems.	TA sees a mixture of learned behaviour as, or from, a parent or adult or from childhood.	Thoughts and actions are controlled by those experiences.
(4) THEORETICAL DYNAMICS	(5) ANALYSIS	(6) VERBALISATION
Fixed patterns of behaviour are established.	The therapist and client role-play as parent, child, teacher, adult, etc. to discover the roots behind actions.	Client and therapist exchange roles to clarify mechanism with appropriate dialogues.
(7) LABELLING	(8) OBJECTIVITY	(9) STRUCTURE
Client is able to label thoughts, feelings and actions with new words.	When labelled, overt behaviour and abstract ideas can be clearly identified.	A new, more accurate, assessment helps client resolve problems.

Those three 'Labels, Objectivity and Structure' are more or less identical as (7), (8) and (9) in all the tables. They are the signposts that indisputably connect every form of psychotherapy *including our Teddy bear*.

The tables can be adapted and equally applied to almost any form of psychotherapy.

Future AI treatment cannot possibly succeed without that one unifying factor. I feel sure similar tables could be drawn to represent AI when we move on to such therapies over the coming years.

REFERENCES

Beck, Judith S; Cognitive Behavior Therapy, Second Edition: Basics and Beyond, Guilford Press: New York (2011)

British Association for Music Therapy, 24 - 27 White Lion Street, London N1 9PD, T: 0207 837 6100 E: info@bamt.org

Claire Harris; Developmental psychology, What is Psychology? (12th March, 2012)

Crane, R.S., Brewer, J., Feldman, C., Kabat-Zinn, J., Santorelli, S., Williams, J.M.G. and Kuyken, W; What defines mindfulness-based programs? The warp and the weft, Psychological Medicine, pp. 1–10 (2017)

Cathy Malchiodi; Art Therapy Sourcebook (Sourcebooks) Paperback (2006)

Mark Twain; Pudd'nhead Wilson's New Calendar, Following the Equator (1897)

Carl Rogers; Client Centred Therapy: Its Current Practice, Implications and Theory Paperback (2003)

Noam Chomsky; Language and Mind 3rd Edition, Massachusetts Institute of Technology, (January 2006)

Vance Oakley Packard; The Hidden Persuaders (1957)

Article on celebrities and their favourite teddies, Daily Mail (7th June 2013)

Woman trying to find lost Teddy's owners, Metro, (30th March 2017)

Report of kind hearted mum and the one-armed Teddy bear lost on the A9; The Scottish Sun, The Daily Telegraph (29th March 2017)

Rufus Bear, The Miami Herald, Fox News, and YouTube (10th January 2017)

Nation of Shopkeepers, World of Bears, The Daily Telegraph (20th March 2018)

Jarrett, C; Feeling socially excluded? Try touching a Teddy bear (seriously). The British Psychological Society Research Digest (21st November 2011)

Llorens; L. Teddy bears accompany 35 percent of British adults to bed, survey says poll. Huffington Post (21st February 2012).

Peterson, C; Did you bring a stuffed animal to college? The Good Life, Psychology Today (4th November 2010).

Sigmund Freud; A General Introduction to Psychoanalysis (1920)

Jean Piaget, John Bowlby, An Introduction to Teddy Bear Therapy: A Systems Family Therapy, Psychology of The Child, Paperback (1972).

Approach to Child Psychotherapy by Leandri Beyers, Warwick D. Phipps & Charl Vorster, Journal of Family Psychotherapy, Volume 28, Issue 4, Pages 317-332 (2017)

John Bowlby; Attachment and Loss: (Penguin psychology) (1991)

D.W. Winnicott; Transitional Objects and Potential Spaces: Literary Uses of (1952),

Sigmund Freud; Fragment of an analysis of a case of hysteria 'Dora': Collected Papers, Vol. 3, pp. 63–64 (1901)

Kidd E, Berkovitz BKB, Phillips C; Winnie-the-Pooh and the Royal College of Surgeons (2016)

Saul McLeod; The work of Lev Vygotsky (2014)

F. Perls, RF Hefferline and P. Goodman; Gestalt Therapy: Excitement and Growth in the Human Personality, Souvenir Press (1972)

Eric. Berne; Transactional Analysis in Psychotherapy: A Systematic Individual and Social Psychiatry (1971).

Corrine Sweet; Our Love Affair with Teddy bears, What is Psychology? (10th March 2012)

Teddy Bear Quotations: Exley publications 1992

D.W. Winnicott; Playing and Reality (1971)

Sigmund Freud; The Interpretation of Dreams, (first published in English 1913)

Sleeping with a stuffed animal as an adult is OK, Psychologists say, Today Paper (6th October 2017)

Nick Bostrom; Superintelligence: Paths, Dangers, Strategies (2014)

Michael Sigman; Cybertherapy Is Cyber, But Is It Therapy? Huffington Post (27th November 2010)

Joan Sotkin; Teddy Bear Therapy, Prosperity Place (13th June 2018)

Richard F. Miniter; Teddy Bear Therapy versus the Mental Health Professionals, American Thinker (16th January 2016)

William Wordsworth; *'The Child is father of the Man'* poem, The Rainbow (1802)

Printed in Poland
by Amazon Fulfillment
Poland Sp. z o.o., Wrocław